4/20/71

D0559425

DATE DUE

TWENTIETH CENTURY
INTERPRETATIONS
OF
MISS LONELYHEARTS

TWENTIETH CENTURY
INTERPRETATIONS
OF
MISS
LONELYHEARTS

A Collection of Critical Essays

Edited by
Thomas H. Jackson

Prentice-Hall, Inc. *Englewood Cliffs, N. J.*

A SPECTRUM BOOK

Current printing (last number):
10 9 8 7 6 5 4 3 2 1

PRENTICE-HALL INTERNATIONAL, INC. (*London*)
PRENTICE-HALL OF AUSTRALIA, PTY. LTD. (*Sydney*)
PRENTICE-HALL OF CANADA, LTD. (*Toronto*)
PRENTICE-HALL OF INDIA PRIVATE LIMITED (*New Delhi*)
PRENTICE-HALL OF JAPAN, INC. (*Tokyo*)

Contents

TWENTIETH CENTURY
INTERPRETATIONS
OF

MISS LONELYHEARTS

Introduction

by Thomas H. Jackson

Miss Lonelyhearts is about despair, alienation, violence, fragmentation, dehumanization, victimization, and sterility—about all of these things as definitive qualities of modern life. And though some of them are more nearly central than others, they are so ineluctably interrelated in the novel that to speak of any one as a "cause" of the others is but an academic exercise. Consequently, the book seems unusually multifaceted and susceptible to differing interpretations, all suggestive, and all at least partly valid, depending on which facet first catches the eye.

In the present collection of essays, for example, Edmund Volpe emphasizes the despair in the novel and West's preoccupation with the loss of what seemed once to be values but are actually illusions. Professors Light and Edenbaum, on the other hand, emphasize in part the hero's interposition of the ego between himself and the Absolute and how this cuts him off from any salvation or even "solution." Yet Arthur Cohen, with a certain validity, can see and say the opposite: that Miss Lonelyhearts is a latter-day "holy fool," like Mishkin in *The Idiot* of Dostoevsky, a man prepared to sacrifice himself for his fellow man, but ignored and therefore disabled by his unappreciative community. Still another cross section through the narrative points to West's consciousness of Freud's theories of human personality; in this light, Stanley Hyman can read the book as an exploration of a kind of derangement of sexual energies in modern America—but always qualified, such is the interrelatedness of West's motifs, by conjunction with other themes, such as the pervasiveness of violence and the anguish of the suffering feminine principle. Robert Andreach pursues a separate but parallel issue in seeing the novel to be concerned with the irrational in general, with the loss of religious values more viscerally grounded in human nature than Miss Lonelyhearts' rather rationalized Christianity, which has driven the irrational cult of Pan underground. Finally— the book has something for everyone, it seems—a reader who is also a professional writer, the late Josephine Herbst, less concerned with interpretation than with another writer's exercise of his craft, writes of the book in terms of its intellectual, technical, and social backgrounds and of the writer's techniques as distinct from what the fiction is saying.

I think it is right to insist on the usefulness of all these approaches, precisely because the novel is such a closely wrought network. Light's discussion of disillusion in the book is inevitably connected with his own perception of the importance of its hero's search for order and of the false order embodied in Betty's simplistic attitudes. When Edmund Volpe suggests that the interposition of the ego, in the form of Miss Lonelyhearts' rock-like imperviousness near the end of the novel, is a necessary *defensive* gesture, the only alternative to an equally ruinous view of the horror of life, the apparent disagreement with Light and Edenbaum is but evidence again of the multifaceted nature of the book: everything is tied to everything else.

Suppose, for example, one begins by considering the motif of order. This branches into all sorts of directions. In the chapter "Miss Lonelyhearts in the Dismal Swamp" Miss Lonelyhearts imagines himself inundated by a sea of civilization's junk; he tries to form the random objects that roll up into a cross, but "every wave added to its stock faster than he could lengthen its arms." Coming as it does after his sexual encounter with Fay Doyle, this phenomenon is not a bad figure for some of the main concerns of the novel. The tendency of the cross to grow toward the shape of a phallus by sheer pressure of mechanical flotsam and jetsam is not just a threatening of the spiritual by the appetitive; it is the threatening of order by disorder, and it is emblematic of a widespread disintegration of human experience. Miss Lonelyhearts' appeals to Christianity are solely on behalf of order; again and again in the novel he refers to it as "the answer" to the misery and moral disorder he sees around him, and hardly at all as a devotional consideration. His invocation of the Christ answer, furthermore, is always conscious, and at one point we are told that its unavailability for Miss Lonelyhearts is due to Shrike's having taught him to handle the Christ myth with a "thick glove of words"—that is, too consciously and too deliberately. It is thus opposed to the "Pan" impulse with which it struggles in the novel. Christ is love, and thus rooted in the irrational, but He is also control and order; Pan is spontaneity, but spontaneity gone bad—riot, violence, chaos. That the invocation of Christ reaches down to activate the lurking Pan-energies in the self reveals how wrong is the sundering of the rational from the irrational that characterizes West's world. The worship of Pan was one way of acknowledging and allowing expression to the irrational in the human psyche; to drive it underground, as Robert Andreach suggests, merely frustrates irrepressible human energies.

The sundering of rational and irrational is intimately related to other troubles in the world of Miss Lonelyhearts. The characters in the book are only half persons or worse and cannot act as whole persons. The men cannot love, and the women could not accept them if they did—consider the reductive emotional outlook of Mrs. Shrike, who cannot join "love" and sex in her mind, or of Mrs. Doyle, who knows sex but not love. As male and female are cut off from each other, the person is cut off from society: Miss Lonelyhearts' colleagues jest truthfully in their speakeasy conversation that the individual's experience cannot be socially meaningful. Even language is disabled: it is words, as we have seen, that spoil the Christ escape for Miss Lonelyhearts. When Peter Doyle attempts to converse with Miss Lonelyhearts, his speech is an incomprehensible jumble "of retorts he had meant to make when insulted and the private curses against fate that experience had taught him to swallow"—that is, language reduced to merely reproducing, not helping to order, a jumble of feelings. Similarly with Shrike, whose conversation is a bitter revelation of moral chaos in its besliming of all sources of order. The letters, though more innocent, are also but a reproduction of the disorder they bring forward for cure. Language, West's novel implies, can be a cry of anguish or a cry of hatred; it cannot be an expression of reason. At no point in the novel does speech or writing function in the service of anything closer to reason than an imitation or burlesque of it.

A moral order presupposes some coincidence of thought and feeling: morality is in part how we feel about what we perceive, how we value it, how we think it ought to be. The divorce of thought and feeling evident in the breakdown of language in Miss Lonelyhearts' world produces violence: emotion divorced from reason or control means chaos and destruction. The same divorce produces the sterility of that world, too: in rational life, fruitful human relationships are not reasoned or calculated merely, any more than they are the egotistical devouring of one human organism by another. But Miss Lonelyhearts' colleagues are to us, as to him, only names. Mary Shrike is only a known source of certain limited sexual satisfaction. Betty he sees only as the embodiment of a point of view. In the relationship between all these people and the world at large, this perverse reductivism takes the form of mechanization. The nonsensical "goat and adding machine cult" that Shrike reads about, whose members feel that numbers are sacred because they are the only "universal" language, is echoed later in Miss Lonelyhearts' gloomy review of headlines in "Miss Lonelyhearts on a Field Trip"—"Mother slays five with ax, slays seven, slays nine . . . Babe slams two, slams three. . . ." In modern America quantity, not quality, counts, and numbers are indeed interchangeable and therefore a universal language. In a hideous age of gadgetry, Miss Lonelyhearts has come a cropper over the truth that the really important ordering power is not the statistical one his culture gives him.

Miss Lonelyhearts, then, is a deflation of the heroic novel whose hero confronts the flux and attempts to order it. The flux, as always, is the world with its cruelties and sufferings. The letters Miss Lonelyhearts is assigned to answer are its expression, and ultimately Fay and Peter Doyle are its embodiment. West's extensive use of the Doyles for this purpose (we shall pursue the implications of his mechanical treatment of them later) takes various forms. Through suggestive and often shared imagery, through echoed speech, and through various conceptual and situational parallels the Doyles and their state become a summary of other characters and situations. Andreach reminds us that the author's bathing Fay in sea imagery during her lovemaking with Miss Lonelyhearts makes her a symbol of fertility of sorts, since the sea can be seen as the source of life; yet it also makes her the very embodiment of a kind of flux and formlessness whose mutations are beyond the control of man—this seems all the more relevant when one recalls the sick vision of the sea and the cross which shortly follows. Miss Lonelyhearts' fixation on the knife and a "battered horn" that "grunted with pain" in the chapter following the lovemaking is pretty clearly a reminiscence of that scene; it also invites association with Shrike's earlier complaint that sleeping with Mrs. Shrike is like "sleeping with a knife in one's groin." Fay's comic-pathetic attempt to seem a victim of seduction makes her a perhaps imperfect approximation to the many women in the novel who are in fact victims of lust and depravity; yet she herself has literally been such a victim, at the hands of the father of her ironically-named child Lucy. She is also in some sense a recapitulation of Mary Shrike and Betty in being simultaneously a victim of human sexual appetites and a narrow-minded wielder of sex for her own purposes.

Peter Doyle is a walking manifestation of the disorder and misrule implicit in a world of flux ("His eyes failed to balance; his mouth was not under his nose; his forehead was square and bony; and his round chin was like a forehead in miniature. He looked like one of those composite photographs used by screen magazines in guessing contests"). He is a Miss Lonelyhearts letter in the flesh, doubly a victim with his lameness and his status as an insulted and then a betrayed husband. And like Fay, he echoes other characters in the novel: in the speakeasy, Shrike "raised his fist as though to strike" Miss Farkis; in the Doyles' apartment at one point Doyle "made as though to strike his wife." His queerly incommunicative speech at his first meeting with Miss Lonelyhearts (later he barks like a dog) is surely representative of the malfunctioning of language endemic to the whole *Miss Lonelyhearts* world. At the same time Doyle is also a version of Miss Lonelyhearts. He, too, according to his letter near the end of "Miss Lonelyhearts and the Cripple," wants to know "what is it all for . . . what in hell is the use day after day . . . what is the whole stinking business for." That he and Miss Lonelyhearts twice end up holding hands is suggestive not of homosexuality, as Hyman says, but of identity—or is it the hero succumbing to one aspect of flux as he has already been engulfed by the other?

The nearly loveless disorder of the Doyles' marriage is but a realization of the disorder of the letters and the self-centered cruelties and neglects they reveal. Neither Fay nor Peter seems much aware of the other as a person ("I am . . . unhappily married to a cripple," Fay writes revealingly; again and again she makes the same depersonalizing categorization: "my husband who is a cripple"; "He's a cripple like I wrote you"; "have to depend on a cripple"; "a shrimp of a cripple." Only twice does she use his name. Doyle himself has internalized his non-identity—"I am a cripple 41 years of age," he writes, "which I have been all my life.") Unwittingly or not, Doyle is his wife's procurer; she insults him and she strikes him—but only after he has threatened to strike her. Their marriage is a little world made as uncunningly as the big one, marred by violence, obliterative of selfhood and dignity, unlovely and utterly beyond the rational control of either victim.

These facts all suggest, then, that we should read the Doyles as, among other things (Andreach and Hyman offer suggestions about the other things), the principle of flux come to life. But they perform their function in a more complicated way as well, a way implied by the title of the episode immediately following Fay's seduction of Miss Lonelyhearts, "Miss Lonelyhearts in the Dismal Swamp." Through the letters, the flux has already wrought a grave spiritual effect on Miss Lonelyhearts; bearing in mind the full sense of the term *spirit,* we may say that the letters are the spiritual manifestations of suffering. The Doyles are its physical manifestation. The effect of Fay Doyle's sexual ingestion of Miss Lonelyhearts is to demonstrate for the only time in the novel what its climate as a whole would deny—unity of soul and body, as Miss Lonelyhearts retires to his bed physically—as well as spiritually—ill. The sum of the episodes with Peter Doyle is but a fatal intensification of this theme. Driven by his spiritual miasma to the physical morass of Fay Doyle, Lonelyhearts succumbs irrevocably to the principle of flux in the figure of Peter, who shoots him. The hero is physically destroyed in the midst of a spiritual fantasy of himself as Christ—an additional irony being that he *is* a Christ; but at this point the narrative yields to the facts of real life: Miss Lonelyhearts is Christ only physically, and his death has no valid spiritual content.

West, I said, "uses" the Doyles. It is a measure of the bitterness in his view of modern life that his version of the heroic plot is expressed through a set of almost purely symbolic characters whose essential claims as persons are undercut and denied by their reductive symbolic values. Obviously a character can be symbolic without being dehumanized; but in West's fable the two go together, and the condition symbolizes his world. His technique becomes an embodiment of his theme in the sense that his people have no being, only symbolic value. Miss Lonelyhearts himself is apprehended less as a character than as a state of mind, or worse, a plight (his name, of course, is not his name, but the name of his public function). As Professor Edenbaum points out in his essay, West originally gave his hero a proper name but replaced it with Miss Lonelyhearts. West sedulously avoids any suggestion that his hero has a realistic inner life, and when he dies we have seen but the completion of a diagram. Late in the novel Betty is reduced to "the party dress," and in fact she is little more than that anywhere in the book: a mere emblem of naive, detached, simplistic (and implicitly self-involved) thoughtlessness. Shrike, the emblem of caustic, cynical disbelief, is a more compelling—and repellent— presence, but he is not really a character in the traditional sense; he is, like T. S. Eliot's Prufrock, a voice, not a person, a category, to be filled in by each reader for himself out of his own experience.

The status of West's characters as non-persons is underscored by their tendency to blur into each other. When Peter Doyle "made as though to strike his wife," he mirrors Shrike, who had made as though to strike Miss Farkis. Miss Lonelyhearts is assimilated to Shrike in his theatrical posing before Betty in "Miss Lonelyhearts and the Fat Thumb," and Betty, perhaps, to Miss Farkis, when she "raised her arm as though to ward off a blow." Likewise, when

Miss Lonelyhearts tries to reconcile the Doyles with unctuous
pieties about strength and love, we cannot help recalling—especially given the novel's brevity—Betty's earlier attempt to stem his
agonized wrath with, "I love you"; from one point of view, then,
the hero becomes momentarily a version of Betty. Furthermore, all
the women in the book are alike in sharing a common torment—
all are seduced, raped, deceived, or otherwise abused.

But if these two strategies underscore West's deliberate dehumanization of his characters by weakening their individual iden-
tities, they can be seen in another light as well. Miss Lonelyhearts
acts throughout the book as though the possible solutions to his
plight were limited by his actual surroundings. For example, he
tries to palm off on the Doyles shoddy pieties that are partly what
he got from Betty and partly what he peddles in his column. He
lives, in fact, in a terribly finite world, and the Christ dream, his
one nonmaterialist escape, is no longer, for him, dreamable, partly
because he is afraid to let himself go and dream it. He applies for
"escape," therefore, only within the dreary limits of the people
around him—Betty, Mary Shrike, the drunkenness of his colleagues,
violence of his own (e.g., against the "clean old man") inspired
by the violence he sees around him, even Shrike's kind of word-
mongering. What is true for Lonelyhearts is true for the world of
the book as a whole. The facts of life are hideous, yet the one
potential universal palliative—dreaming—has been discredited by
deceitful, grasping, cynical, and powerful men, who treat the
less powerful as starfish treat oysters. With no way to turn except
to turn on each other, these people find themselves trapped in a
world of terribly limited possibility. Perhaps this is the significance
of the book's grim and mechanical comedy about women's breasts.
Miss Lonelyhearts sits with Betty and toys casually with her breasts;
he sees a White Rock poster and notices the girl's breasts and how
the nipples resemble tiny hats; he spends an evening trying not
to be bored by glimpses of Mary Shrike's breasts, and when he
takes her home he stands with her in the hallway and kisses them
—more or less passionately; his, and the reader's, attention is fixed
on Betty's breasts as she hangs clothing to dry at the Connecticut
farm. Stanley Edgar Hyman finds Freudian significance in all this

breast-consciousness, but is it not rather a reiteration of the gloomy finitude of Miss Lonelyhearts' world? It is as though for him woman equals breast—and while the source of this reductivism may be psychological, its symbolic value in the novel is not; it is an emblem of rigidity, a symbol of sad limits. Even psychologically the ruinous consequence of fixation is that it prevents the realization of alternative possibilities. That a man is fixated on his mother is, by itself, insignificant; the loss is that the fixation prevents his attaining other more creative and rewarding kinds of relationship. This is the meaning of the figures of abused and suffering womanhood with which the novel abounds. Almost without exception in this novel, female suffering real or imagined stems from the repression of women to purely sexual potentialities. Mrs. Doyle has been reduced to an object of sexual pleasure by her Italian businessman; Betty is left at the end of the novel pregnant, a victim of Miss Lonelyhearts' detached sexuality; the first letter in the book comes from a woman who has been reduced to the status of pleasure-and-child-machine by her husband's sexual appetites combined with his religious "convictions." The next letter but one tells of a thirteen-year-old girl who has been raped. The most telling case of all, perhaps, is the jocularly brutal discussion of lady novelists in the speakeasy, where Miss Lonelyhearts' colleagues decide that all lady writers need "a good rape"—which would presumably cure their presumably unwarranted urges to ascend into the realm of the imaginative, there to exercise a potentiality other than that conventionally allotted to women. And this is surely West's point: the world is designed—and if it is not designed, the men in it will see to it that it gets designed—to limit the function of women to one and only one thing. It is not necessary to adduce the traditional literary use of women as symbolic of potentiality, or salvation through passivity, or fruitful irrationality, or the surrender of dominion and the sublimation of ego, though there are various well-known analogies to what West is doing here—Sonia, for one, in *Crime and Punishment*. As with women, so with Christ and the slaughtered lamb in Miss Lonelyhearts' dream: none of these, apparently, will subsist quietly and dependably—and narrowly—as the men in the book want them to; they are constantly threatening to break out into unwanted (unknown and therefore frightening) potentialities. The dilemma of West's world, then, is two-fold: human energies and potentialities are confined and repressed within an agonizing and horrifying finitude; and yet something in these people drives them to *enforce* this finitude, to disable or eradicate any agency that seems to offer a way out. Why this should be raises some interesting questions about West's writing and its relationship to the times in which he lived.

Those times included two great landmarks in the emotional and psychic history of the United States, the economic boom of the 1920s, and the Great Depression of the 1930s. After *The Dream Life of Balso Snell*, West's first and least worthwhile novel, his books focused on the popular mythology of democratic capitalism, its effect on the lives of his fellow citizens, and its major instruments for propagating the faith—*Miss Lonelyhearts* fixes on the advice column dodge, *The Day of the Locust* deals with Hollywood-movie-house culture, and *A Cool Million* satirizes Horatio Alger. In all these books West sees the commercial spirit to be in absolute control of American life, and he sees it to be the father of lies. In *Miss Lonelyhearts* the "dream" has been betrayed, betrayed by agencies with a stake in its betrayal and in replacing it with pre-packaged, over-the-counter fantasies—for the dream is freedom; the dream is inner, private, uncontrollable, and never made anyone a dime. West's three last novels depict a world that has been reduced to the coarsest materialism, but which is constantly being foisted off on people as not materialistic, a world in which the commercial movie magazine is offered in lieu of dreams, the commercially motivated newspaper columnist in lieu of spiritual adviser, phony nightclubs in lieu of pleasure gardens. For such a world to survive, of course, delusion is a crucial necessity. It only adds to the irony that West's characters, like the denizens of any Inferno, help forge the chains that keep them from the truth.

The vulgarization or betrayal of the dream is an old theme in American literature—one need only recall Mark Twain—and as a child of the 'twenties West must have been thoroughly alive to it: this was the decade that dressed up the "profession" of real-estate peddling in the non-word *realtor,* canonized Henry Ford, and deified the businessman, proclaiming with a smug naiveté at least as old as the days of Flaubert that thanks to modern commerce the millennium was at hand—and it culminated in the soul-wrenching revelation of the depression.

The time of the writing of Miss Lonelyhearts was an excited period, when American literature seemed about to go places, when a great deal of romanticism surrounded the idea of being a professional writer, and when many serious writers were deluded into thinking they could do honest and creative work in the promising medium of films. We know now that American literature did not go anywhere special; the romanticism of the intellectual or creative life has largely vanished, what with government and academic grants and positions, and as for films, one can only say that up to now no first-class literary talent has ever been allowed to function fully in that baldly commercial air. At any rate Nathanael West was very much of that climate. Specifically American writing he saw as a kind apart, and so did the artists around him—witness, for example, the last paragraph of William Carlos Williams' review of *Miss Lonelyhearts* in this collection. Whatever West may have felt about the quality of modern American life, moreover, he seems to have been willing to see the artist trim his sails to its wind, praising the short "lyric" novel as better suited to American life than more agglutinative styles. I bring this up because of the peculiar kind of appeal that *Miss Lonelyhearts* seems to make. It is a book many people discover, with delight, in college, and it seems then the perfect expression of creative writing as part of a truly intellectual life style. Yet it is also a book that tends not to be reread over the years: few who first read it in college will have reread it ten years later, though they will remember it as an "exciting" book.

One reason for the neglect which tends to follow upon one's admiration for the book is its deliberate economy. Compared to more ambitious works it seems narrow and therefore less of an achievement and certainly a less inclusive imitation of human life. But this narrowness is a part of its success. There are, as has already been noted, no interesting people in West's book, no elab-

orate situations, whether narrative as in Dickens, structural as in
Doris Lessing, or psychological as in Dostoevsky or even Hemingway. *Miss Lonelyhearts* cultivates a spareness daring in its intensity
and the result is an astonishingly successful economy of means.
West was a child of the first really great age of American gadgetry,
and *Miss Lonelyhearts* reflects an odd faith in mechanical de-
cisions. West's own comments on the book ("Some Notes on Miss
L.," in *Contempo* early in 1933) speak much in terms of mechanics,
and of writing as the deliberate application of premeditated mechanical principles. Thus he toys with the idea of using comic strip techniques in a novel, then does just that in *Miss Lonelyhearts* (see
The Fiction of Nathanael West, by Randall Reid, in the Selected
Bibliography and see below, pp. 93–96, for an excerpt from that
work). He theorizes about the propriety of short novels as such,
then produces a very short novel. ("Leave slow growth to the book
reviewers," he writes, "you only have time to explode.") He theorizes
further that "Psychology has nothing to do with reality," and
therefore in *Lonelyhearts* eschews it, except for "cases" from William James and E. E. Starbuck. West speaks, in fact, of using the
findings of psychology the way one might use mythology, as a
compendium of *types* or *emblems,* the way Euripedes "uses" Hip-
ploytus to depict the type of one-sided man, or the way Sophocles
"uses" Oedipus to create an emblem of overweening self-confidence.

This manner of West's reminds one of the techniques of other
writers more or less of his day—the Imagists, William Carlos Williams, Ezra Pound: a whole generation of writers whose work was
directed by what Hugh Kenner has called "an aesthetics of
glimpses," which involved stripping expression down to its barest
essentials. Behind Pound's commitment to the poetic moment as
subject matter and determinant of technique lay a complicated
set of ideas about the role of subjectivity in art and the nature
of the reality art recorded, and these ideas issued in remarks like
"Beauty is a brief gasp between clichés" and in an art characterized
by an austere economy: "Dichten = Condensare," he wrote in the
ABC of Reading. West did not share Pound's aesthetic, but he
knew a version of it in the admired work of his colleague Williams,

and he could write, "For a hasty people we are too patient with the Bucks, Dreisers and Lewises . . . Forget the epic, the master work. In America fortunes do not accumulate, the soil does not grow, families have no histories." Such an attitude exemplifies what I have characterized as the romanticism of West's ambience. So sentimentalized a view of the anxiety-laden bustle of the American life-style would hardly find public utterance in intellectual circles of today. The contrast between this and West's bitter contempt of the commerce-ethic is striking in the extreme, and further exemplifies, perhaps, that readiness to make an intellectual silk purse out of a substantial sow's ear so typical of the period in which he worked. Again, we may compare Williams' use of Paterson and New Jersey in his own *magnum opus, Paterson.*

The novel as an institution has certainly gone on to other things since West's day, and it is doubtful that he would have had much more influence than he has had even if he had not died so young; his technical experiments were simply not that radical or far-reaching. In this he is like rather than unlike his countrymen, for it is arguable that the really seminal experiments in the form of the novel have not been carried out by Americans. Melville, Hemingway, Dos Passos, Faulkner, West: all are writers who consciously forged new forms useful to themselves only. Yet of West's vision of American life, who today can truthfully say that it was wrong? The apocalyptic riot at the end of *The Day of the Locust,* which enacts the violent upheaval implicit in *Miss Lonelyhearts,* has not taken place in quite that form. But we have the gruesome memory of Chicago in 1968, of southern (and northern!) university campuses since 1960, and of the perpetration of individual hideousness we do not lack examples. As these words are being written, a young army officer is said to have wantonly slaughtered single-handed more than a hundred Vietnamese villagers, including many women and children ("Officer kills eighty, kills ninety . . ."). Perhaps in their willing use of napalm, gas, and bombs in remote Asian villages the descendants of the *Miss Lonelyhearts* world are finally having a chance to exteriorize the hatred, the violence, the blood-lust, the destructiveness West always said was in them.

West's life was short; it was ended by a traffic accident, one of
those events of random violence he saw as endemic to the American experience. It was an unremarkable life, or at any rate remarkable only for its resembling so closely the cliché idea of the
life of the young writer in the 'twenties and 'thirties in America.

His real name was Nathan Weinstein; he was born in New
York City in 1903. His father, an immigrant from Russia, became
a prosperous building contractor—and then, thanks to the stock-
market crash, a ruined building contractor. West went to public
schools in Manhattan, where, like many writers more gifted than
he, he was a fairly bad student. He was even worse at the DeWitt
Clinton High School, which he left without graduating. Nonetheless, he was at Tufts University a year later, admitted on the
strength of a high school transcript belonging to one Nathaniel
Weinstein that credited him with roughly half again as many
courses as he had actually taken or passed. (See James Light's
Nathanael West: an Interpretative Study, and Jay Martin's *Nathanael West: the Art of His Life* for detailed scrutiny of these
events. These books are presently the major sources for such information.) After two months West was "advised" to withdraw (not
because of the doctored transcript, apparently), but the following
semester found him enrolled at Brown University—this time as
Nathan Weinstein. He seems to have resumed his real name so
as to make use of the academic transcript of some other Nathan
Weinstein at Tufts in order to transfer into Brown. (The odd
talent that enabled West to obtain—twice—such documents for
his own use remains a puzzle for posterity to unravel.) At any rate
he became a serious student at Brown, and, by all accounts, a
cliché college boy of the 'twenties, courting the fraternities, drinking heavily, dressing sharply ("like a well-heeled mortuary assistant," according to a college friend), and socializing in the intense
way that until recently formed a central feature of the mythic
conception of college life in America. He seems to have found himself intellectually as well; he read widely, in courses and out; he
tried his hand at writing; and some of the literary judgments he
formed at Brown he was still maintaining years later—his dislike,

for example, of "long-winded Scandinavians" and the sprawling novels of Dreiser.[1]

He graduated from Brown in 1924—after just two and a half years. He had lived the role of College Boy and had worked his way toward the role of Writer; naturally he must now go to Paris, and he did. He lived there for two years, dabbling in the cliché behavior of the literary life. To speak of him as living by stereotypes is not, I hasten to add, to ridicule him or jeer at his insincerity. On the contrary; West is more than a little reminiscent of F. Scott Fitzgerald in the utter naiveté with which he pursued these various roles. Reading the remarks of his friends, one gets the feeling that for West these stereotypes represented real achievements, and there is no evidence during these early years that he pursued them with anything but complete sincerity. To that extent his life seems representative of a peculiarly American sort of sentimentality.

When he returned to New York he took a job as assistant manager of a hotel which was to provide his livelihood for the next six years. As night manager he had time to work on his writing while he worked for the hotel, and he was further able to help out needy writers—among them, Dashiel Hammett and James T. Farrell, who came under West's permissive wing as unregistered guests at the hotels where he worked. In retrospect this seems the very type of non-job for a young writer, a job at which he can preserve his anonymity and his integrity and remain in some sense free for creative work; yet towards the end of his stay West clearly hated the life. He completed his revisions of *The Dream Life of Balso Snell* during these years and had it privately printed in 1931. It fell dead from the presses, but it introduced the name "Nathanael West" to the world.

At this time West was also extending his friendships in the literary world of New York: Quentin Reynolds and S. J. Perelman he knew from college; Hammett, Farrell, Edmund Wilson, and William Carlos Williams he had met in the city, and also Josephine Herbst, to whom he was introduced by Williams and who became

[1] See West's "Some Notes on Miss L." in *Contempo* 3 (May 15, 1933): 1–2.

his most eloquent and most gifted spokesman. As his literary con-
tacts grew, so, not unexpectedly, did his desire to get out of the
hotel business. In 1932 he and Williams founded a new version of
a defunct literary magazine called *Contact,* and he finally gave up
his job at the Hotel Sutton and went to live and write in the
Pennsylvania countryside, near Josephine Herbst's farm in Erwinna.

The publication of *Miss Lonelyhearts* in 1933 was a pathetically
spoiled triumph. The book was very favorably reviewed, but the
publisher went bankrupt before it was properly distributed, and
by the time West obtained another publisher, the reviews were
forgotten and the book a dead issue. His agent, however, sold it
to Hollywood, where West signed on as a writer with Twentieth-
Century Fox. *Miss Lonelyhearts* was "adapted" into a cheap and
tawdry movie, and West, in a few months, was back in Erwinna.
This was not a happy time for him. Just after his Hollywood ar-
rangement collapsed, so did his relationship with a middle-class
Catholic girl he had hoped to marry—doubtless in the hope that
she would put the seal on his escape from Jewishness. On the other
hand, he became editor of another little magazine, *Americana,* and
the next summer (1934) published *A Cool Million.* Unfortunately,
this book too was tepidly received, and West spent the next few
months turning out a series of unmarketable short stories while
his mother filled his ear with praises of the reliability of the hotel
business. The drifting which followed the appearance of *A Cool
Million* took a new form in early 1935, when he got another Hollywood job—this time with Republic Studios, the most commercial
film-makers of the day. Though it was clearly hack work under-
taken to free himself for real work, not all the films he worked
on were contemptible. He even made a tentative movement toward
Broadway, but the only play of his that was performed closed
after two showings. In 1938, three years after returning to Hollywood, he published *The Day of the Locust,* certainly his most
ambitious and probably his most considerable novel. It, too, met
a mixed reception, and never sold over 1,500 copies in West's
lifetime.

The Depression, which had so colored the outlook of *Miss
Lonelyhearts,* worked as well on West's political sympathies. He

was pretty thoroughly leftist by the time he arrived back in Holly-wood; he joined the Screen Writers Guild, and he was among the signers of the manifesto of the American Writers Congress in 1935. One wonders, given the cynical bitterness that pervades West's novels and the feelings implied by his politics, what romantic or sentimental compulsions kept him flitting moth-like around the streetlamps of Hollywood and, briefly, Broadway, those two capi-tals of moneymaking so thinly disguised as centers of art. One thinks of Joyce in his Berlitz classrooms, of Eliot in Lloyds bank, of Pound in his poverty, and the comparison is not to West's credit. Is there a specific kind of American artist who can only be convinced of his success when it is reflected in wealth?

In 1940 West married and went off on a long honeymoon which was to be also a period of gestation for a new book. But driving home later that year from a Mexican hunting trip, he missed a stop sign and ran into another car. An hour later he and his wife were dead. He was 37. The story of the collision, replete with errors, was reported on the movie page of the *New York Times.*

NOTE: In all of the essays in this collection except Prof. Light's references to *Miss Lonelyhearts* use the pagination of *The Complete Works of Nathanael West* (New York: Farrar, Straus, and Cudahy, 1957). I have accordingly deleted from the individual essays all footnotes to this effect [ED.].

PART ONE

Interpretations

The Christ Dream

by James F. Light

Miss Lonelyhearts, like all of West's novels, is episodic. The narrative pattern is similar to that of *Balso Snell*. Though the tone of cynical mockery in *Balso* changes to the fevered religiosity in *Miss Lonelyhearts*, both novels tell of a search. The search is for some spiritual reality to believe in and live by, and in both novels the search ends in tragic disillusionment.

Miss Lonelyhearts tells the story of a young man who writes a sob-sister column for the newspapers. Miss Lonelyhearts (in the original manuscript West had named his hero Thomas Matlock) gives advice in his column to desperate and helpless people who have no other place to turn. Miss Lonelyhearts has taken the job as a joke, and he hopes it will lead to his writing a gossip column. After a while the pathetic letters addressed to him make him feel that the joke has turned upon him. Here the novel really begins, and the action treats Miss Lonelyhearts' attempts to come to terms with his own helplessness. This he can do in no easy way. Instead he must go through what might be called a program for the attainment of salvation. This program, or pilgrimage, eventually leads to a mystical experience, but by the time it has reached this culmination Miss Lonelyhearts has become completely alienated from those around him; in the eyes of the world, he has become "sick." Though tragically ironic, it is only fitting that he

"The Christ Dream." From Nathanael West: An Interpretative Study, *by James F. Light (Evanston, Ill., Northwestern University Press, 1961), pp. 74–98. Copyright © 1961 Northwestern University Press. Reprinted by permission of the publisher. [Page references are to the 1933 New Directions edition of* Miss Lonelyhearts—*Ed.*]

should be killed by one of those desperate creatures who have led him to his ordeal and his mystical experience. The novel, as West claimed, is the "portrait of a priest of our time who has had a religious experience."[1] The portrait is painted in a succinct, imagistic style, and it attempts to fulfill West's claim that

> Lyric novels can be written according to Poe's definition of a lyric poem. The short novel is a distinct form especially suited to use in this country. France, Spain, Italy have a literature as well as the Scandinavian writers. For a hasty people we are far too patient with the Bucks, Dreisers, and Lewises. Thank God we are not all Scandinavians.
>
> Forget the epic, the master work. In America fortunes do not accumulate, the soil does not grow, families have no history. Leave slow growth to the book reviewers, you only have time to explode.[2]

From the point of view of Miss Lonelyhearts, this priest of twentieth-century America, the American scene is a desolate one. Its basic components are decay and violence and pain. In this American wasteland, the decay is extreme. Though the action takes place in the spring, the air seems waxy and artificial, while the dirt of the city appears without possibility of generation. Even in the country, the vision is of death and rot. For Miss Lonelyhearts, the entire world is dead, and only through hysteria, brought on by the name of Christ, can the "dead world take on a semblance of life" (p. 39).

In this decayed world, violence exists everywhere. Partly its source is the Darwinistic struggle for survival; partly it stems from the unsatisfied spiritual needs of man. Through violence, modern man comes alive; it is the salt by which he savors an existence without the Saviour. Before attaining grace, Miss Lonelyhearts thinks that "only violence could make him supple" (p. 49); or, comparing himself to a dead man, he feels that "only friction could make him warm or violence make him mobile" (p. 79).

Man is caught in a viselike trap: in a sterile world he would still be alive, but only through violence can he feel himself potent.

[1] Nathanael West, "Some Notes on Miss Lonelyhearts," *Contempo* (May 15, 1933), p. 2.

[2] *Ibid.*

The world of *Miss Lonelyhearts* is, therefore, filled with violence. Its everyday presence is suggested by innumerable actions and images and by casual understatement. "Violent images are used to illustrate commonplace events. Violent acts are left almost bald." [3]

Man's desire for life leads to his seemingly instinctive preoccupation with sexual violence, the type most intimately associated with life. The letters to Miss Lonelyhearts are permeated with sexual suffering, from the nightmarish epistle of Broad Shoulders to the pathos of Sick-of-it-all, who writes that she is expecting her eighth child in twelve years "and I don't think I can stand it. . . . I cry all the time it hurts so much and I don't know what to do" (pp. 13–14). Miss Lonelyhearts' newspaper associates gain vicarious life from the violence of the sexual gang-shag tales they love to tell. Even Miss Lonelyhearts at one time tugs sadistically at a woman's nipples, at another time tears at an unwilling woman's clothes.

This emphasis on violence was in every novel West wrote. Even before the publication of *Miss Lonelyhearts,* West stated his defense:

> In America violence is idiomatic. . . . What is melodramatic in European writing is not necessarily so in American writing. For a European writer to make violence real, he has to do a great deal of careful sociology and psychology. He often needs three hundred pages to motivate one little murder. But not so the American writer. His audience has been prepared and is neither surprised nor shocked if he omits artistic excuses for familiar events.[4]

In this world of decay and violence man is able to exist only through dreams. The search for a dream to believe in is right— and in this contention *Miss Lonelyhearts* and *Balso* agree—for it is only through dreams that men can fight their misery. However, the commercialization and stereotyping of man's dreams have led to a weakening of their power, a puerility in their content. This is the worst betrayal of modern man.

Typically betrayed is Mary Shrike, the wife of Miss Lonelyhearts'

[3] *Ibid.*

[4] Nathanael West, "Some Notes on Violence," *Contact* (October, 1932), p. 132.

chief tormentor. In her early childhood she has been familiar with violence and suffering, but she romantically transforms her past when she speaks of it. Her alterations of reality make Miss Lonely-hearts realize that "People like Mary were unable to do without such tales. They told them because they wanted to talk about . . . something poetic" (p. 90). This desire for the beautiful attracts Mary to El Gaucho, and it is her poetic longing which explains the medallion she wears between her breasts. Both suggest romance, but both are obvious fakes. El Gaucho, with its romantic atmos-phere, is but a commercialized dream, just as the medallion has no religious significance but is an award for a childhood racing contest. These small dreams are betrayals of man's true spiritual needs, but despite their limitations Mary must cling to them. Through such fantasies she attempts to satisfy her psychological need for mystery and romance. Her need unites her with the un-fortunate correspondents who seek help from Miss Lonelyhearts.

Perhaps even more than the letter writers, Mrs. Shrike needs the help of Christ, the Miss Lonelyhearts of Miss Lonelyhearts. Not really able to believe in her tiny dreams, she, nevertheless, needs something on which to dream. The split personality which results can be seen in her inner conflict. On the one hand, she is pulled by the head's knowledge and fears; on the other, she instinctively reacts according to the body's desires. When Miss Lonelyhearts kisses Mary, she reacts with sexual grunts and scents; but never will her mind allow her to submit wholly to the sexual act. Be-cause of the body-mind conflict, with the fears of the mind in eventual control, she will not sleep with Miss Lonelyhearts and cannot respond sexually to her husband. Being divided, Mary can submit totally to no one, and paradoxically one must give oneself to gain oneself. Mary becomes the eternal virgin; and the head, or reason, is the villain that makes her so. Rationalism dooms Mary, and much of modern man, to dream the small dreams rather than the big Christ dream; but the small dreams are psychologi-cally inadequate to the spiritual needs of man.

A more powerful dream might have saved Mary by giving her a mystery and romance worthy of belief. But in this commercialized world the needs of the spirit have been betrayed. The modern dream merchants do not offer love as the dream by which man can conquer suffering. They do not even justify human suffering by stating that it is Christ's gift to man and that by suffering, man comes to know Christ. Instead they offer the easy Technicolor evasions (from Art to the South Seas) that man so much wants to believe in. Unfortunately none of these escapes is powerful enough to salve for long the pain of existence.

In this world of decay and violence and pain, man can react in only a limited number of ways. He can, like Mary Shrike, who wavers between acceptance and non-acceptance of a lesser dream than Christ, become a split personality. By distortion and simplification, he can so blind himself to the suffering of man that he is capable of accepting a lesser dream. He can reject all dreams. He can accept the Christ dream of faith and universal love.

Miss Lonelyhearts' girl friend, Betty, follows the second of these paths. By her excessive simplification of the world, she is able to bring order out of chaos. When Miss Lonelyhearts first thinks of her, he muses "that when she straightened his tie, she straightened much more" (p. 49). Later on, when Betty visits Miss Lonelyhearts while he is ill, she puts the jumbled confusion of his room in order. This same ability to put her universe in order leads Betty to an inner peace that is reflected even in her physical smoothness. Because of Miss Lonelyhearts' own unsuccessful attempts to attain this harmony, he feels Betty is a Buddha, lacking only the potbelly.

For Miss Lonelyhearts, Betty's order is a false one. It excludes not only suffering but also the spiritual needs of man. It degrades man to a mere body and assumes that all his ailments can be cured by such drugs as aspirin. Still, while basically false, Betty's ability to limit experience allows her to retain her innocent, natural speech, and laugh. Such naturalness is more related to the primal simplicities of nature than to the elaborate artificiality, both physical and psychological, of the city. Inevitably Betty combats Miss Lonelyhearts' spiritual sickness by taking him to the zoo and talking of the country's sounds and smells. Then she takes him to the country. Though the visit does not cure Miss Lonelyhearts, Betty becomes an "excited child, greeting the trees and grass with delight" (p. 135).

Betty's vision of the way of the world is one of childlike order and harmony. It is akin to one of the childhood memories of Miss Lonelyhearts:

> One winter evening . . . he had . . . gone to the piano and had begun a piece by Mozart. His sister left her picture book to dance to his music. She had never danced before. She danced gravely and carefully, a simple dance yet formal . . . As Miss Lonelyhearts stood at the bar, swaying slightly to the remembered music, he thought of children dancing. Square replacing oblong and being replaced by circle. Every child everywhere; in the whole world there was not one child who was not gravely, sweetly dancing. (pp. 64–65)

Such a world of simple patterns, however, is the world of childhood only; that it is based on children's limited, and therefore false, experience is suggested by what immediately follows: an unjustified punch in the mouth from a stranger loosens one of Miss Lonelyhearts' teeth. Violence and suffering exist in the real universe, and any harmony which eliminates these elements is false.

Though Betty's world is one of Buddhistic blindness, it can, through its limitations, become a universal of personal love, of "his job and her gingham apron, his slippers beside the fireplace and her ability to cook" (p. 52). This simplification makes Betty oblivious both to the world of suffering humanity and to the things of the spirit. The possibility of such a limited outlook continuing throughout life is slim.

Because the dreams sold by the modern dream merchants offer no adequate solution for conquering or justifying suffering in a world of rot and violence, some cynical sophisticates react toward dreams in still a third way. They reject all dreams. Shrike, Miss Lonelyhearts' chief tormentor, has made such a rejection. So have most of the newspaper men with whom Shrike associates. Once these men had felt that their devotion to Beauty and self-expression justified their existence, but under the commercialized mold of the news story they have lost all faith in Beauty. Shrike, as feature editor, has especially seen culture and Beauty and self-expression corrupted by commercialism. The loss of faith in Beauty deafens these men, whom Shrike epitomizes, to the call of any faith. Mechanically and cynically, they make jokes of man's dreams about the soil, the South Seas, hedonism, and Art. The biggest joke, however, is the Christ dream, and Shrike reserves his most brutal attacks for man's aspirations toward Christ. Shrike sends a parodied prayer to Miss Lonelyhearts:

> "Soul of Miss L, glorify me
> Body of Miss L, nourish me
> Blood of Miss L, intoxicate me . . ." (p. 11).

Or Shrike makes vulgar jokes about Christianity: "I am a great saint. I can walk on my own water" (p. 31). Or Shrike reads and shows others a news story concerning a condemned robber and murderer for whom a goat-and-adding-machine service, a religious ceremony, is to be held. Shrike proclaims that such a service embodies the true American religion. This assertion shows that Shrike has become dominated by the lust of the goat and the mechanicalness of the adding machine. To Shrike man is a thing of chemistry alone.

Except about the sexual reluctance of his wife, Shrike is as emotionless as a machine. His lack of emotion dominates the chapter entitled "Miss Lonelyhearts and the Dead Pan." The dead pan refers to Shrike's lack of facial expression, but the word *pan* also suggests the dead nature-god of flocks and pastures. In Shrike, *Pan* is dead, and Shrike is identified with the new mechanical world based on the emotionless physical sciences. These sciences, in their purest form, exist in the "triangles" of mathematics, and these triangles are symbolized in the novel by the triangular, hatchet-like face of Shrike. These triangles, representing the physical sciences with their tendency to destroy the world of spirit, perpetually bury themselves, as Shrike does, in the neck of mankind.

Shrike's lack of emotion determines his action throughout the book. He laughs at humanity by laughing at the pathos of Doyle. He invents a game which has laughter at the letters of the helpless as its purpose, and that game indicts him as the inhuman joke-machine he is. This lack of love and pity justifies the name Shrike, suggestive as it is of the bird that impales its prey upon a cross of thorns. Shrike has become the anti-Christ, crucifying those who strive for faith.

The final alternative to the inadequacy of modern dreams is to attempt the Christ dream which was once capable of alleviating man's suffering. Miss Lonelyhearts attempts this dream. Puritanical in appearance, he has a "bony chin . . . shaped and cleft like a hoof" (p. 18). The boniness connotes the man of spirit rather than flesh. The cleft chin indicates the split between the spirit and the flesh, between the devil and the saint. This opposition creates barriers to the Christ dream, and they crop up at every milestone of the spiritual journey.

One of the basic obstacles is materialism. Early in the novel Miss Lonelyhearts, like Shrike, accepts the idea of a materialistic and indifferent universe. He feels that if there were some spiritual manifestation, he could show his contempt by casting a stone. But in the indifferent sky there are "no angels, flaming-crosses, olive-bearing doves, wheels within wheels" (p. 25). Wanting to escape from a world dominated by decay and pain, a creation without spiritual manifestation, Miss Lonelyhearts, in true Shrike fashion, starts for a speakeasy.

Two other similarities between Shrike and Miss Lonelyhearts stem from materialism. Like Shrike, Miss Lonelyhearts attempts to become a worshiper of the flesh. Though without great enthusiasm, Miss Lonelyhearts pursues Betty and Mrs. Shrike. Later, he experiences a sexual act with Mrs. Doyle, who embodies primal, carnal, sealike sexuality, and when it is over, he knows that for him flesh-worship is no escape. A more important similarity between Shrike and Miss Lonelyhearts is that for a while Miss Lonelyhearts too attempts to become a joke-machine by laughing at his own sympathetic heart. For Miss Lonelyhearts the laugh is at first bitter and then dies in his throat. It is no wonder that West changed an early draft of the manuscript, in which he had Miss Lonelyhearts express the indictment of escapes found in "Miss Lonelyhearts in the Dismal Swamp," and placed the indictment where it really belonged: in the mouth of Shrike.

Materialism, with its corollaries of carnal love and cynicism, is no solution to Miss Lonelyhearts' need for an answer to the letters. Because of the failure of materialism, Betty, with her faith in personal love and a benevolent, therapeutic nature, finally succeeds in persuading Miss Lonelyhearts to go with her to the country. Momentarily he is able to accept Betty's limited world, but only momentarily. Violence quietly insists upon its existence, for in the country Miss Lonelyhearts sees in stark relief the ever-present animal struggle for survival. The ignorance and viciousness of man also persist; they are personified in the bigotry of a garage attendant who proclaims that it is not hunters but "yids" who have driven the deer from the countryside. Once back in the city, Miss Lonelyhearts realizes that "Betty had failed to cure him . . . he had been right when he said he could never forget the letters" (p. 145).

The ultimate barrier to the realization of the Christ dream is neither Shrike's materialism nor Betty's simplified world. That barrier is pride, and it resides in Miss Lonelyhearts as in all men. Its simplest manifestation is in man's revulsion from his fellow man, his unwillingness to lick lepers, as the saints of old had licked them, out of sheer humility and love. Though Miss Lonelyhearts "wants to lick lepers" (p. 62), he finds it difficult to attain sufficient humility. Rather than uniting himself to the unfortunate, he pities them. The first time he achieves identification is with the cripple, Doyle. The embodiment of broken humanity, Doyle has a primitive pathos that is totally repellent. When Miss Lonelyhearts, striving for complete humility, touches Doyle's hand, he instinctively "jerked away, but then drove his hand back and forced it to clasp the cripple's . . . he did not let go, but pressed it firmly with all the love he could manage" (p. 171). With this handclasp Miss Lonelyhearts symbolically licks his first leper.

This humility leads from the acceptance of Doyle, who represents suffering humanity, to the faith that some order, some pattern, does exist in the universe. There follows an interior calm so perfect that it seems either that of the dead man or of the religious fanatic who, in the perfectness of his faith, is in full accord with his universe. Miss Lonelyhearts' monastic retreat from the world further likens him to the ascetic religious. His asceticism, however, is clearly of the modern world: he not only drinks water and eats crackers but also smokes cigarettes. Still, his is a sainted calm, resting on the "rock" of Christlike love and faith. Miss Lonelyhearts has achieved a life-in-death serenity, where "what goes on in the sea is of no interest to the rock" (p. 194).

Christlike love and faith become the rock which leads to Miss Lonelyhearts' alienation from the sea of life. No longer is Miss Lonelyhearts bothered by intellectual problems such as the existence of pain and violence in a world created by a benevolent God, or the lack of order in a universe which, were it created by a purposeful God, should have order and harmony. The philosophic drama of the novel grows primarily from the first problem, but the lack of visible order has also affected Miss Lonelyhearts. He develops a need for order that he himself sees borders on insanity. He recognizes the sad truth that "Man has a tropism for order. . . . The physical world has a tropism for disorder" (p. 115). Man's intellect is constantly frustrated. Its human limitations make the mind unable to see the infinite order, yet its desires toward God demand that it seek a significant pattern. Philosophically Miss Lonelyhearts justifies his futile search: "All order is doomed, yet the battle is worth while" (p. 116).

Though the battle of the intellect is worthwhile in its direction toward the infinite, it is only by faith, by the abdication of the intellect, that the infinite order is perceived by man. Through humility Miss Lonelyhearts attains this simplified outlook. Now nothing remains of Miss Lonelyhearts save love and faith. Through humility he has united himself to suffering humanity, has accepted a universe whose order he cannot comprehend, and consents to marry Betty. The loss of all things save love and faith leaves "his mind free and clear. The things that had muddled it had precipitated out into the rock" (p. 204). After Betty tells him she is pregnant, he shows no emotional response and asks no questions about the future. In his faith, his loss of intellectual questioning, he can become the kind of person that Betty wishes him to be and can accept a future life circumscribed by her innocent but limited dreams: personal love, children, a farm in Connecticut.

Through his humility Miss Lonelyhearts has become dead to this world. Following Christ's injunction that whosoever would find his life must first lose it, Miss Lonelyhearts can now attain a mystical union with God. Transcending the fevered sickness of his body through a transforming grace of light and perfumed cleanliness, he becomes "conscious of two rhythms that were slowly becoming one. When they became one, his identification with God was complete. His heart was the one heart, the heart of God. And his brain was likewise God's" (pp. 210–211).

In this moment of hallucinatory ecstasy the cripple, Doyle, rings Miss Lonelyhearts' doorbell. Miss Lonelyhearts, wishing to succor with love all the desperate of the universe and expecting to perform a miracle by which the cripple will be cured, runs rapturously toward Doyle. But there is no miracle. Instead Miss Lonelyhearts is shot by Doyle, destroyed, like Christ, by the panic and ignorance of those whom he would save. Doyle, and in him suffering man, shatters the only solution to the intolerableness of man's pain, destroys the Christlike man who perceives that love and faith are the only answers to man's pain in a universe he cannot understand.

True belief in the Christian answers, however, rest upon the dissolution of the self and the subsequent mystical experience of God's love and grace. Until such experiences (the price of which is alienation from this world), the very name of Christ, as Miss Lonelyhearts had felt before his "sickness," is a vanity on the lips of man. After God's love and grace, the personal ecstasy they bring is a "reality," but the reality is incommunicable. Dramatically West pictorializes the division of man from man when Miss Lonelyhearts runs toward Doyle with love in his heart, while the cripple, filled with hatred, makes his way up the stairs. In the ironic lack of communication, Doyle's gun, the symbol of a mechanical, loveless world, goes off, and the two men roll down the stairs together.

Although Doyle is the actual murderer of Miss Lonelyhearts, Betty is also indirectly responsible. She comes in while Miss Lonelyhearts and Doyle are grappling, and Doyle feels she is cutting off his escape. He tries to get rid of his gun, but in his panic at seeing Betty he causes the gun to explode. The involvement of Betty is meaningful, for Betty's fragmentary view of the universe would leave out pain and violence. With her belief that man's needs are always bodily ones and his ills are easily cured by aspirin, Betty would destroy the spiritual in man. Her approach to life would negate the need for Christ. It would kill the Christ dream, for without pain and violence there is no need for the relief of Christ-like love, no need for faith to reconcile unjustified suffering with the existence of a good God.

Betty's fragmentary view is false and cannot endure. Witnessing the murder of her unborn child's father, she will need an even greater blindness than she has shown before if she is to disregard the existence of violence. The pain of childbirth, which West emphasizes in the novel, will impress upon her the fact of suffering. It is inevitable that the childlike innocence and order and calm of her universe must disappear. Then she, like so many others, will have to reconcile pain and violence with a godly universe. Though there are answers that bring no peace, the love and faith of Christ are the only solutions in which man can rest. The Christian answers could make for a better world, one founded on Dostoevsky's Christianity. In a world of lesser dreams than Christ, where, iron-ically and tragically, it is almost impossible, if not completely im-possible, to live by the message of Christ, each pilgrim must find an answer for himself. Miss Lonelyhearts' pilgrimage is over; Betty's has just begun.

In its fusion of form and content, *Miss Lonelyhearts* is the best novel West was ever to write. To the novel nothing should be added and nothing could be taken away. Its stark simplicity of language and sentence structure, a bareness achieved by continual pruning and sharpening through six revisions of the novel, creates a pecu-liarly nightmarish etching of shadows and decay unlike the art of any other American novelist. In addition the book has a warmth, a compassion, which exceeds that of West's other novels. The warmth is especially apparent in the increased depth with which West treats the dilemma of humankind in its need for a dream. Earlier, in *Balso Snell,* West had implied that the wisest thing man can do is to accept himself as an animal and to avoid dreams com-pletely, for in dreams there is only misery. Such an attitude was naïve: an oversimplified solution of a very young man. In *Miss Lonelyhearts,* West probes deeper. The horror of a life lived without any dream is illustrated by the joke-machine called Shrike. Terrible as it is, even a bad dream is better than no dream at all, and this idea, from *Miss Lonelyhearts* on, is constant in West. Faye Greener, in West's last novel, *The Day of the Locust,* puts the insight most bluntly: "She said that any dream was better than no dream and beggars couldn't be choosers" (p. 60). Undoubtedly it would be better for mass man if he wanted a worthy dream instead of the nonsense offered to him by Hollywood or love story magazines, just as it would be better for him to like great art rather than the trash he prefers. His tragedy is that he doesn't make intelligent choices, and he doesn't because of what he is. The pathos of his need to dream, while forced by his nature to choose dreams that will not soothe his pain, is explored with both horror and compassion in *Miss Lonelyhearts,* and in *Miss Lonelyhearts,* unlike *The Day,* the pity is greater than the horror.

While *Miss Lonelyhearts* is wholly unique, one cannot leave it without being aware of how much West is indebted to other writers. Most important are the influences of Dostoevsky, the French Symbolists, and the French surrealists. None of these influences is surprising and least of all is the shadow of Dostoevsky. West himself would have quickly admitted this influence, a fact noted by John Sanford's comment that West had a constant "little brag that he could rewrite Dostoevsky with a pair of shears." [5] Josephine Herbst also remembers from her conversations with West the numerous discussions of Dostoevsky: the way West commented on the impact and power of *The Possessed,* with its grotesqueness and its violence; how Stavrogin's rape of a young child tormented West as it tormented Stavrogin himself.

In *Miss Lonelyhearts* the strong Dostoevskyan influence is apparent in the character of Miss Lonelyhearts: he reads and ponders Dostoevsky; he wears the same hair shirt of guilt that tortures so many of Dostoevsky's heroes; he wears the hair shirt because he, like Dostoevsky's heroes, feels his inability to aid the helpless of the

[5] John Sanford, "Nathanael West," *op. cit.* [*The Screen Writer* (December, 1946).]

universe. Another Dostoevskyan concept is the dualism of good and evil which tugs at the heart of Miss Lonelyhearts and which fills him with the dream of attaining the love and humility of Christ and at the same time permits him sadistically to twist the arm of the clean old man.

Dostoevsky's influence on West is also shown in a letter West once wrote. In it he stated his conviction that the survival of humanity depended upon its acceptance of the Christian ideals of Dostoevsky.[6] This Christianity is probably best defined by Dostoevsky himself when he says: "If we do not follow Christ we shall err in everything. The way to the salvation of mankind leads through his teachings alone." [7] This is to say that whatever reservations he might have about whether God created man or man created God, Dostoevsky had no reservations about the perfect love and humility which Christ preached and lived. West understood Christ and his teachings in just the same way.

Whether West believed in the probability of man's free survival, however, is open to doubt. Always in West's writing, and above all in his last novel, there is the fear that there may be truth in Dostoevsky's "Legend of the Grand Inquisitor" in *The Brothers Karamazov*. In Dostoevsky's masterpiece, the Grand Inquisitor charges that God has given man not happiness but freedom. This freedom only the few can bear; for the many it leads only to untold suffering. The Grand Inquisitor, by enslaving man, has taken the burden of freedom from his shoulders; he has given man the semblance of earthly happiness even though at the cost of eternal joy.

In *Miss Lonelyhearts* and the novels which followed, this same freedom causes the suffering of West's characters. They strive for something to worship completely, yet never find anything which will wholly enslave them. There is no Grand Inquisitor in West's world to give the mass of men earthly happiness by giving them total enslavement. Most men are thoroughly contemptible creatures, doomed to misery, without a nature capable of choosing a dream worthy of dreaming. In their misery West's creatures turn to mere

---

[6] Information in a letter quoted in an unpublished paper by Richard Gehman, "Miss Lonelyhearts and the Surrealists."

[7] Quoted in Rene Fuellop-Miller, *Fyodor Dostoevsky* (New York, 1950), p. 56.

parodies of something to worship. In the world of the Grand Inquisitor, Christ at least exists as an attainable ideal for the few who
can worship Christ by their own free choice. In West's world there
is no such possibility. For the modern world, the big dream, the
Christ dream, is just an ironic joke. Few men can even conceive of
such a dream. He who dares to dream it dies clutching with Christ-
like love the cripple, who is man, in his arms; but the darer dies in
the most meaningless of ways, killed accidentally by a mechanical
thing in the hands of the cripple he would save.

The French symbolist influence upon *Miss Lonelyhearts* mani-
fests itself generally in the bareness and concentration of the action
and the writing, as well as in the epigrammatic style and satiric
manner. In addition certain of West's ideas are more common perhaps to French symbolism than to any other literature: for instance the flesh-spirit opposition, or the concept that the world
is a hospital or a madhouse from which man cannot escape save
by death. Villiers de l'Isle Adam, one of the symbolists whom West
discussed with Saul Jarcho, uses both concepts in *Axël:* though
Axël and Sara, at the end of the play, may have dominion over
every earthly desire, they prefer to escape by suicide from this
world of flesh and pettiness. Joris-Karl Huysmans, to whom West
refers in *Balso*, dramatizes both ideas in *Là Bas.* Huysmans' major
character, the writer Durtal, wants to escape the humdrum, to get
out of the world,[8] and Huysmans' villains, Marshall Gilles de Rais
and Mme. Chantelouve, are satanists whose evil stems from the
same out-of-the-world desire.[9] (The latter phrase is repeated often
in the novel.) Durtal, however, learns, through a sexual rendezvous
with Mme. Chantelouve, "that the flesh domineers the soul and
refuses to admit any schism." [10] Therefore, the out-of-the-world
dream is but a fantasy for either the religious or the satanist. At
the end of the novel the hero of the people, the demagogue Bou-
langer, wins political victory. A little group listens to the fleshly
beast, the people; they hurrah for their champion, and one of the

---

[8] J. K. Huysmans, *Là Bas,* trans. Keene Wallis (Evanston and New York, 1958),
p. 101.
[9] *Ibid.*
[10] *Ibid.*

group comments that such hurrahs would not greet those that
might really help the agony of the people—a sage, an artist, or a
saint. Listening, Durtal sees "whirlwinds of ordure . . . on the
horizon!"

> "No," said Carhaix [a simple, religious man], "don't say that. On
> earth all is dead and decomposed. But in heaven! Ah, I admit that
> the Paraclete is keeping us waiting. But the texts announcing his
> coming are inspired. The future is certain. There will be light . . ."
> Des Hermies [a doctor interested in satanism] rose and paced the
> room. "All that is very well," he groaned, "but this century laughs
> the glorified Christ to scorn. It contaminates the supernatural and
> vomits on the Beyond. Well, how can we hope that in the future the
> offspring of the fetid tradesmen of today will be decent? Brought
> up as they are, what will they do in Life?"
> "They will do," replied Durtal, "as their fathers and mothers do
> now. They will stuff their guts and crowd out their souls through
> their alimentary canals." [11]

The Symbolist whom West's writing most reflects is Charles
Baudelaire. The influence of Baudelaire's prose poem "Anywhere
out of this World" is clearly seen in *Miss Lonelyhearts*.[12] West's
reference to the poem in *Balso Snell* indicates that West knew the
poem well. Its influence in *Miss Lonelyhearts* is especially apparent
in the chapter "Miss Lonelyhearts in the Dismal Swamp." Baudelaire's poem compares life to a hospital in which all the patients
long to change their beds. In the poem Baudelaire and his soul
discuss the question of moving elsewhere. To his soul, Baudelaire
suggests various possibilities of escape: Lisbon for its warmth, Hol-
land for its tranquillity, Batavia for its tropical beauty, Tornéo, the
Baltic, the Pole. To all of these escapes the soul is silent until at the
end of the poem it explodes: "N'importe où! pourvu que ce soit
hors de ce monde!" In almost exactly the same way Shrike offers
escape to Miss Lonelyhearts: the South Seas, Art, Hedonism, Suicide, Art, and Drugs. At the very last, Shrike mockingly offers the

---

[11] *Ibid.*

[12] West's indebtedness to Baudelaire, and specifically to the prose poem "Any-
where Out of This World," is treated at some length in Marc L. Ratner's
"'Anywhere Out of This World': Baudelaire and Nathanael West," *American
Literature* (January, 1960), pp. 456–63.

escape of Christ. It is after Shrike's mockery that Miss Lonelyhearts most desperately strives for the love and humility and faith of Christ. His growing involvement with the Christian dream leads to his alienation from the rest of the world, his mystical experience, and eventually his death. Ironically, the big dream will not work in this loveless world, and so can only lead *out of the world.*

Most important to the eventual impact of *Miss Lonelyhearts* are the images that West creates. These images owe a good deal stylistically to the surrealists—probably more than West himself realized. The nihilistic side of surrealism wished to destroy the world of rationalism, to replace it with the surrealistic world of individual perceptions. This world at its most truthful was the product of dreams and visions. The rational relationship of objects was replaced by the subconscious and truer vision, where Dali clocks hung without suspension in vari-colored skies, where an umbrella and a sewing machine copulate on an operating table, where the symbol of the surrealistic is the *sur réalité* of the objects in a drug store: douche bags piled against aspirin bottles and both outlined against a toothpaste ad. In this kind of surrealistic perception, suggestive of the cosmic chaos, the surrealists felt that there was a shocking humor, the humor of the Jacobean writer of conceits. It is this kind of humor, destroying the stereotyped perceptions, laughing at the normal human relationships, that the surrealists strove for in their work. This humor of conceits is shown in Picabia's painting of "A Young American Girl in a State of Nudity," in which the girl is portrayed as a clean, dry, spark plug. It was even better illustrated by Dali, who painted a pair of scales to fulfill a teacher's assignment to paint a Gothic virgin. When the teacher expressed astonishment, Dali replied by saying that although others might have seen a virgin, he saw a pair of scales. This same desire for conceits led to the search for new images in literature, for the revolution of the word that Eugene Jolas preached so often in *Transition.* The revolution was to be accomplished by new arrangements of words, and the search for the new sometimes led to strange literary amusements: for instance, some writers plucked by chance, out of a paper bag or a newspaper, two or more words and then yoked them together to create a shocking effect.

The chance combinations eventually bore fruit in such weirdly titled, surrealistic poetic texts as "L'Homme Approximatif," "Mouchoir de Nuages," and "Les Vases Communicants," such a startlingly titled painting as Dali's "Debris of an Automobile Giving Birth to a Blind Horse Eating a Telephone."

This metaphysical humor of conceits is at the root of West's macabre wit in *Miss Lonelyhearts*. Even the basic concept suggests the metaphysical in its yoking of Christ to an advice-to-the-lovelorn columnist. The progress of Miss Lonelyhearts toward his "sickness" leads to distorted, unique perceptions: a man's tongue is seen as a fat thumb, and a man's cheeks as rolls of toilet paper; a woman's buttocks are seen as enormous grindstones and a woman's nipples as little red hats; a woman is seen as a tent, veined and covered with hair, and a man as a skeleton in a closet; the stone shaft of a war memorial becomes a penis, sexually dilated and ready to spout seeds of violence.

As a writer, West took great pride in his image-making ability. His pictorial eye was active as far back as college, where he spent a good deal of time drawing. His interest in painting lasted throughout his life, and shortly after college he began his collection of Max Ernst's surrealistic prints. That West was proud of the images he created is evident in his statement that *Miss Lonelyhearts* is indebted for its psychology to William James's *Varieties of Religious Experience*, but "The immagery [*sic*] is mine." [13] This pride in his imagery is again evident in his statement that he had originally intended to subtitle *Miss Lonelyhearts*

> "A novel in the form of a comic strip." The chapters to be squares in which many things happen through one action. . . . I abandoned this idea, but retained some of the comic strip technique: Each chapter instead of going forward in time, also goes backward, forward, up and down in space like a picture.[14]

In these imagistic terms the characters subordinate to Miss Lonelyhearts become merely simplified states of mind. Juxtaposed pictorially against the growing alienation of Miss Lonelyhearts

[13] West, "Some Notes on *Miss Lonelyhearts*," p. 2.
[14] *Ibid.*, p. 1.

from the world of reality, the minor characters serve primarily
as contrast and chiaroscuro. This static, pictorial quality is also
true of the actions, which seem like candid snapshots of people
caught in mid-air against a background of dull sky and decaying
earth. Each action becomes a symbol of an abstract state of mind
and heart, and leaves one remembering a series of almost inde-
pendent pictures rather than with a memory of the developing
actions: Miss Lonelyhearts bringing the knife down upon the lamb;
Miss Lonelyhearts twisting the arm of the clean old man; Miss
Lonelyhearts entwined about Doyle while Betty watches the two
roll down the stairs. The pictures are, in reality, sensory portrayals
of the inner heart and mind of Miss Lonelyhearts. They portray in
archetypal imagery Miss Lonelyhearts' guilty mind (the murder of
the lamb); his self-torturing, flagellating heart (the beating of the
clean old man); his deluded, mystical vision (the entwined pair).
In West's hands the case histories of James and Starbuck and
Freud become merely the necessary folklore tradition, the Bullfinch, that instigates him not to psychologize but to pictorialize.
This pictorialization, West felt, was the writer's fulfillment:

> Psychology has nothing to do with reality nor should it be used as
> motivation. The novelist is no longer a psychologist. Psychology can
> become much more important. The great body of case histories can
> be used in the way the ancient writers use their myths. Freud is your
> Bullfinch; you can not learn from him.[15]

This use of Freud as the inspirer of images revealing states of
heart and mind is continually apparent in the novel. A simple illus-
tration is the deliberately sinning mind of Miss Lonelyhearts which
envisions sex as a way of escape from the letters and then involun-
tarily pictorializes the sex act in the tent-and-skeleton image of Mrs.
Doyle. In a more extended way, this imagistic style is shown in the
description of Miss Lonelyhearts' feeling that in sex is the core of
pain: a mental state objectified in Miss Lonelyhearts' image of
himself

> in the window of a pawnshop full of fur coats, diamond rings, watches,
> shotguns, fishing tackle, mandolins. All these things were the parapher-

[15] *Ibid.*, p. 2.

nalia of suffering. A tortured high light twisted on the blade of a
gift knife, a battered horn grunted with pain. (p. 115)

Later on this imagistic, surrealistic style is evident in the externaliza-
tion of Miss Lonelyhearts' feeling of himself as a rock unaffected
by the sea of life. Miss Lonelyhearts visualized that

> a train rolled into a station where he was a reclining statue holding
> a stopped clock, a coach rumbled into the yard of an inn where he
> was sitting over a guitar, cap in hand, shedding the rain with his
> hump. (p. 188)

Or again this use of Freud as Bullfinch is suggested in Miss Lonelyhearts' inner sensation of himself as a dead man, in a world of dead
things, being reborn through grace. The feeling is pictorialized in
the vision of

> the Christ that hung on the wall opposite his bed. As he stared at it,
> it became a bright fly, spinning with quick grace on a background
> of blood velvet sprinkled with tiny nerve stars.
>
> Everything else in the room was dead—chairs, tables, pencils,
> clothes, books. He thought of this black world of things as a fish.
> And he was right, for it suddenly rose to the bright bait on the wall.
> It rose with a splash of music and he saw its shining silver belly.
> (pp. 209–210)

These images make the abstract concrete. They pictorialize the
inner feelings. They partially explain the peculiar power of West's
writing, with its nightmarish involvement in a world of hallucina-
tions and shadows. In this approach to writing, West owes a good
deal to surrealism. In the success with which he makes his distorted
world of half-light come alive, perhaps more alive than the world
of everyday toast and tea, he is indebted only to the intensity and
power of his own imagination.

Nathanael West

by Josephine Herbst

In the '20s, the youthful generation lived in the shadows of the Great War; they walked on earth trembling with the reverberations of the Russian Revolution. Signs in the sky flashed forebodingly, prophetically; they warned, they beckoned. No year, no week in the '20s was like any other; it was all flux and ferment with artistic movements evolving to political positions; political situations breeding tension and fission. The avant garde was diversified, intransigent, revolutionary. One contingent extolled the machine; others saw it as the great neuter, abstracting man. The air was filled with voices, in accord and at war with one another. But basically there was unanimity; *to see* at all cost, to refuse to sink in the trivial mirage of day-by-day. If the youthful generation repudiated the betraying parental institutions, they were jubilant orphans seeking their unafraid ancestors who had dared to go below where the demons breed. The truth was the concrete. Don't deal from the deck of generalities; don't pretend you hold the Queen of Hearts when all you have is a spade or club. Don't brag, don't bluff; that's for the business man out for the fast buck.

This was the intoxicating climate West shared in Paris; its momentum was powerful and contagious. In spite of the crash of 1929, the year West began *Miss Lonelyhearts,* the climate continued to prevail; it carried over into the '30s. It was a prime factor in the élan which carried West through, stimulating his sense of the audacious, shooting out rays to repel, to attract. What was innate in him was solid; he stood apart from his contemporaries; he was

"Nathanael West" by Josephine Herbst. From Kenyon Review *(Autumn, 1961). Copyright © 1961 by Kenyon College. Reprinted by permission of the author and publisher.*

also of the company. . . . The impetus which had evolved in a variety of new art forms of the epoch took its more immediate shape among the futurists, both Italian and Russian, as well as in the cubist forebears of the surrealists. The Italian manifestoes of 1906, the Russian "Slap in the Face of Public Taste" of 1912, aimed at the gleeful demolition of the old for the sake of the innovating new, and predated Dadaism. In carrying destructiveness to its absolute emptiness, Dadaism had petered out in abstractions. But shortly before West came to Paris, the movement had detonated to surrealism. Both Dadaism and surrealism were undoubtedly potent liberating antecedents for West.

West's deviations from the surrealists are significant. He was with them in pursuing the reality which lies beyond what we call real. He shared—with limitations—the revolutionary element in surrealism which was twofold: it was a revolt of the psyche, against the authority of reason; it was also an appeal to reason to liberate man from his oppressors—family, church, fatherland, and boss. In their utter rejection of the whole conception of bourgeois living for the sake of the mystical idea—*le merveilleux*—the surrealists faced a dilemma. The genii in their Pantheon were Freud *and* Hegel. Pulsing for infinity, in aching concord with impossibilities, the surrealists made a universe always diminishing. Hegel rescued them from gross inwardness; their conception of the human soul evolving like everything else in nature gave a dynamic role to man in the universe. The conflicting tensions between events and internal pressures transformed Breton's homemade formula *Changez la vie!* to Aragon's Marxist position: *Change the world.*

West never ventured beyond the accusatory. More in the vein of Diderot or Stendahl he accepted man as he found him. The one loophole in West's condemned universe that admits a possible ameliorative vision is in *Miss Lonelyhearts.* In its Westian setting, Miss Lonelyhearts' vision of Christ is among the company of the surrealist impossibilities.

Doubtless the clue to the unique quality in the fiction of Nathanael West lies more in what he recoiled from than in what he embraced, but face to face with the man who was also the artist he radiated more of what he liked than what he rejected. In the early fall of 1932, when William Carlos Williams urged John Herrmann and myself to "look up young West," we drove straight from Rutherford to the Hotel Sutton in Manhattan to find him. This tall slim young man with the warm handclasp and infectious smile was the author of *Balso Snell,* and it was no surprise. His composure, his quick repartee, his sudden silences, resounding like a pebble dropped into a well, suggested the complexities, the contraries to be found in the work. He could hand you a drink with the grace of someone offering you a rose; could stand at ease, listening, with the aristocratic air of detached attachment. He could flash and blaze; then, suddenly, you were looking at the opaque figure of a man gone dumpy, thick, who might be brooding behind a cash register in a small shop on a dull day.

We three had dinner together that night in West's hotel and talked as though we had been the oldest of friends. The little magazines of the '20s, published abroad, provided the contiguity for us all. By 1930 they had faded; *transition* was gone; *The Little Review, This Quarter* had folded. Ford Madox Ford's *transatlantic* had given up earlier; the American *Dial,* a more sedate cousin to the intransigeants, had ceased in 1929. *Secession, Broom,* Pound's *Exile* were out or on the way. We had been indoctrinated by the infectious internationalism of the epoch; what went on in Berlin, Rome, Paris, or Moscow was news from home.

The material for the new young writers, however, was not foreign but strictly indigenous. Edward Dahlberg had written *Bottom Dogs* in Brussels; its introduction was by D. H. Lawrence; its content, both in matter and idiom, was pure American. Published in 1930, it preceded by five years *A Cool Million* in exposing the underbelly of the American dream; there was nothing soft about that belly; it was cinder-hardened, work grimed, flayed yet vulnerable. Dahlberg's anti-hero never achieves even the communion of the rabble horde in *A Cool Million;* a lone individualist, he attempts to dislocate the implacable materiality of his situation, but he is a piece of that materiality, its bone and marrow, experiencing no more than a simple and frightening "being there." The heavy weight of *things* pressed hard upon both Dahlberg and West; the response of each was expressed in reliance upon a unique and flexible use of words for the articulation of the inarticulate. West's affinity with the Faulkner of *As I Lay Dying,* also a publication of 1930, rests in the sense of the comic which both writers used to invest their submerged characters with a crackling livingness. None of these writers uses intellectuals as characters; any attempt to deal with abstractions issues only in the concrete; there are not even any young Nicks up in Michigan. They carry the work of words to a sub-level where non-communicating man is the most lost of the lost; where objects warn, threaten, or console. In the year that gave the Nobel Prize to Sinclair Lewis, the books of both Faulkner and Dahlberg were remaindered. But for the intransigent youth of the '20s, Lewis had never been anywhere except in limbo.

The public and the work of the new young writers were far apart. But, behind the wall, a sympathetic telepathic connection made an in-world for the "outsiders" that was viable. Letters, meetings, chance encounters identified one of the "elected" Unelect. The proposal to drink *Bruderschaft* upon a first acquaintance was not an empty gesture; it indicated apprehension of a longed-for brotherhood. It was a period when impulse was not literary fiction but actual. On the impulse we urged West to come with us to our place in Bucks County the following day. He had confided that he had been working on the book to be called *Miss Lonelyhearts* for three years; later he divulged that he had been carrying in his pocket a marriage license to wed his fiancée for the same length of time. It was delirious autumn and for three days we barely slept. We walked through fields of tall grass, plucked the antlered horns of red sumac, talked of Pushkin for whom autumn had been the creative season. We drank Pennsylvania bootleg rye and homemade red wine; read aloud Carl Sternheim's *A Pair of Underdrawers,* recited poems by Hans Arp, "the trap drummer," and Schwitter's *Revolution in Revon.*

John Herrmann had an autographed copy of George Grosz's *Ecce Homo;* he had known the artist in Germany. We opened the big volume flat on the table, poring over the grotesque comics of the violent Berlin world. We spoke of his *Christ in a Gas Mask,* which had been banned in Germany. Grosz's vision of Christ was of the universal common soldier martyred in the Great War; he himself had been a pacifist who had feigned insanity to avoid induction. The love Miss Lonelyhearts yearns for in his vision of Christ has a similar source; its roots are in humanity, not in a definitive God-seeking. But West's new novel had already taken its final shape before he came to the country where he was shortly to engage a room in an old hotel to complete the work. Taunted with, "If autumn could be the great creative season for Pushkin, why not for you?" he had decided to ask for leave-of-absence from the Hotel Sutton, had picked up our challenge to finish the book, *now or never*.

A comparison of the chapter called "Miss Lonelyhearts on a Field Trip," as it appeared in the magazine *Contact* for October 1932, with the final version, indicates the minute but important particulars which West picked at to the last moment. The extreme tensions in West, which he sought to resolve in his prose, make for finicky writing. Compared with *Bottom Dogs* or *As I Lay Dying* there is a delicate precision in *Miss Lonelyhearts* paradoxical to his violent material. His method may be apprehended in a comparison of the two versions. For instance, he changes "junk that had been made precious by memory" to "junk that memory had made precious." He adds an occasional telling phrase. In "Well, how's the drunkard: Goldsmith asked." he turns the period to a comma, adds, "imitating Shrike." In the sentence "He fastened his eyes on two disembodied genitals copulating" he strikes out "copulating," doubtless at the publisher's insistence. He alters "poppa" to the more American "papa." But the most significant changes are in the names. In this scene Miss Lonelyhearts encounters the fatal Doyles; the wife who will betray him to the husband; the husband who will deny Miss Lonelyhearts his Christ-like role. The *Contact* version gives the name of Mrs. Doyle's child as Mary. West wisely alters it to Lucy. Doyle is called Martin in *Contact;* Martin becomes the more significant Peter, the disciple who denied. At the end of this chapter, when Miss Lonelyhearts has capitulated to the overpowering Mrs. Doyle, the sentence in *Contact* reads: "She rewarded him with a kiss, then dragged him limping to the bed." West cut "limping" as too obvious an identification of the psychic cripple, Miss Lonelyhearts, with the physical cripple, Doyle.

West's belated revision of the key names, Mary and Peter, as well as other interior evidence, indicate that his conception of the role of Miss Lonelyhearts as a seeker of Christ evolved more from the impulse to find love within humanity than to find God. James Light asserts categorically that West understood Christ and his teachings as Dostoevsky did; he substantiates his claim by a letter West once wrote stating his conviction that the survival of humanity depended upon its acceptance of the Christian ideals of Dostoevsky. But exactly what is meant by "Christian ideals"? You might say that Dostoevsky saw all mankind caught in eternal conflict with what he defined as the law of the ego and the law of self-sacrifice. Deeply aware of the duality of man's nature, agonized by inner conflicts, Dostoevsky saw man on earth aspiring toward an ideal in opposition to his nature; this ideal was no less than bringing his egoism in love as a sacrifice to mankind or another creature. For Dostoevsky there was only one sin; failure to fulfill the positive and ultimate ethical ideal of free sacrifice of the individual. Dostoevsky never knew the calm faith or smooth-flowing love that he constantly calls for in his books. He wanted faith; but a demonic lucidity kept him at the edge of grace. He questioned himself and the sacred texts and discussed instead of accepting dogma. The religious impulse in Dostoevsky fused with social-political ideas of his period; the *Underground Man* may be seen as a rebuttal to the rational-egotism of Cherneyshesky, who voiced the aspirations of the social revolutionaries of the period. But Dostoevsky vetoed the Socialist ideal as the logical extension of the worship of Baal initiated by Western capitalism; he refused to believe that we sacrifice our lives for logical proofs, or even material well-being: "It is for a living internal spiritual image with which well-being is linked, or for the truth of our own nature, or for a dim presentiment of a future vital image for which a logical deduction has respectfully opened the door."

His superior penetration into moral, metaphysical, and aesthetic problems did not prevent Dostoevsky's political views from being the less Chimerical and Utopian. His views of the role of the Russian Muzhik are messianic and sentimentalized; in America the social-revolutionaries of the '30s were to sentimentalize "the worker."

West sentimentalized no one. In his detachment from the prevailing climate of the '30s he refrained from Utopias but he shared the emotions which could produce a version of the free sacrifice of individuals in Silone's *Fontamara* and Malraux's *Man's Fate*. But West's concern for the world stopped with a delineation of its dire predicament; in the severity of his vision he condemns mankind to a deterministic cycle as completely as the adherents of economic-determinism but without their futuristic goal.

The movement in *Miss Lonelyhearts* from imprisoned within to the prison without brings no victory. The will to love humanity is ironically in vain. Miss Lonelyhearts is made definitely concrete; he is the son of a Baptist minister to whom, as a boy, the vision of a snake arises when he shouts the name of Christ. In Miss Lonelyhearts the suppression of the forbidden leads to disgust and guilt. His cloven chin in combination with his high puritan brow and thin nose are the concrete representations of his duality. His longing for a unified self pushes up from the subconscious; he takes the Christ from the cross of his crucifix and nails him, a lone man, on the wall. The cross is the symbol of the eternal duality in man from which Miss Lonelyhearts seeks escape. He is an empty bottle in a world of doorknobs. As he approaches his mystical vision he becomes the insensate rock; the eddies swirl around him. When he proposes to Betty she is "a party dress" and he behaves in the male version of a Hemingway heroine: "He was just what the party dress wanted him to be: simple and sweet, whimsical and poetic, a trifle collegiate yet very masculine." His seeking takes secular form; he does not pore over Holy Writ but studies the words of Dostoevsky's Father Zossima about loving humanity.

This sad moralist was by intention a satirist, but he offers no positive idea; if his novels signal "beware," they present no prospect either within the self or in the world beyond an engulfing moment. What he shared with Dostoevsky was a horror of the emptiness of sterile intellect, a hatred of dogma. He shared a Dostoevskian compassion which prevented him from creating any actual villains in his vision of a world ruled by the villainy of the little.

The Possibility of Belief:
Nathanael West's Holy Fool

by Arthur Cohen

Throughout West's work there runs a single-minded preoccupation with the character of "the holy fool." This theme has a long
history in Western religious thought, an especial history in Russian
religious thought, and a unique history in the work of Dostoevsky.
From the unworkable plan for a novel to have been called *The Life
of the Great Sinner,* Dostoevsky developed *The Brothers Karamazov*
and subsequently *The Idiot* and *The Devils.* In each of these, elements of the same dialectic emerge: the opposition of the perfect
sinner and the perfect saint. Dostoevsky was sensitive to the diffi-
culty of making such characters authentic and believable. Raskolnikov, Ivan, Smerdyakov, Stavrogin, Kirilov emerge on one side;
Sonia, Alyosha, Prince Myshkin on the other. The conditions of
the Russian world: poverty, oppression, drunkenness, were the
elements of external relief. The protest was not, however, against
the degradation of the physical and social world, but against the
impoverishment of the inner life of man, the void of inner truth.
The effort of Dostoevsky was to relocate the varieties of human
feeling and authenticity, to restore the possibility of sanctity.

In West the problem of "the holy fool" remains, though its
statement and nuance are different. America in the thirties posed
different problems than Russia in the sixties and seventies of the
last century. Unlike their Russian nineteenth-century counterparts,
the American intellectuals and artists were already in rebellion and

---

*"The Possibility of Belief: Nathanael West's Holy Fool" by Arthur Cohen.
From* Commonweal *64 (June 15, 1956), 276–78. Copyright 1956 by the Commonweal Publishing Co. Reprinted by permission of the publisher.*

alienation. The objective order had witnessed the triumph of industrial bureaucracy, the dislocation of personality, the fragmentation of the social order. Dostoevsky was a prophetic novelist, anticipating what was to be in the objective order, as it had already emerged symptomatically in the inner life of man. There is no question but that the spirit of man records more quickly and sensitively what emerges but gradually in the social order. Man usually knows, long in advance of his destruction, that he is being destroyed. It is Dostoevsky's uniqueness to have ascertained the consequence of man's disorder and to have described it. He is prophetic in the same sense that we recognize Kierkegaard, Burckhardt, and Nietzsche to be prophetic.

West, on the contrary, anticipates nothing that is to come. It is his merit to have described with unbelieveable clarity the destruction that has passed, the pestilence that has visited us and has been invited to stay. The power of *Miss Lonelyhearts,* the ineffectualness of *A Cool Million,* and the more elaborate structure of *The Day of the Locust* result from the fact that the deterioration of the American world, West believed, was accomplished. The savageness manifest in *Miss Lonelyhearts* could become more subtle and exploratory in subsequent novels; West could return to questions of form because there was no longer any urgency to the problem. As desperate as *Miss Lonelyhearts* indubitably is, it is perhaps more optimistic than his later novels. For by the time of *The Day of the Locust,* West's anguish had settled and become tolerable.

Miss Lonelyhearts, the male writer of an advice column, has a solution to the horror of the world: it is what he calls "the Christ complex." The Christ complex is precisely a complex, not a belief in specific documents of faith, not faith in any order of sacrament or scheme of salvation. It is a complex, a fixation of the mind, a conviction that only if Miss Lonelyhearts himself becomes the shoulders of the world, the bearer of man's suffering, the kisser of lepers, restorer of bodies, nurse-maid to the suffering and distressed; will humanity be healed.

In *Miss Lonelyhearts* the primary text is taken from Father Zossima of *The Brothers Karamazov:* "Love a man even in his sin, for that is the semblance of Divine Love and is the highest love

on earth. . . . Love the animals, love the plants, love everything . . . you will come to love the whole world with an all-
embracing love."

Miss Lonelyhearts, however, does not love the world. He is dis-
gusted by the world, sensuality, his own body and passion. The
contempt for the physical is hazed by liquor and rhapsodized by
that mental liquor of the ascetic deceiver, the egotism of suffering.
He must force himself to love, to take upon himself more and more
of the world's anguish even at the sacrifice of all of himself, of the
sanity which enables man not only to love completely, but wisely.
Needless to say, his "Christ-complex" destroys him, for it deludes
him. He misrepresents the world and is martyr to his misrepresen-
tation.

In *Miss Lonelyhearts* West attempted to make a statement of
what happens to "the holy fool" in the modern world. He is not
treated as a mad saint and revered for his sanctity and the divinity
of his madness. He is misunderstood and destroyed. It is not that
he is either saint or fool, for, in West's view, he is a victim of the
world he seeks to love, fragmented by the broken world he wishes
to mend. He misapprehends the world because he is not capable,
as modern man is generally not capable, of maintaining any distance from the world, any perspective or quiet before it. . . .

The holy fool is ultimately defeated. The saint can communicate
only when there is a community to address, when people are at
least bound by common affections and belief, when they share
sources of feeling and devotion. The saint cannot speak when absolutely nobody listens. He may live and die, known to God, but such
secret sanctity will not allow us to praise, witness, or follow him in
his way. Miss Lonelyhearts, Lemuel Pitkin, Homer Simpson are
defeated by their self-deception about the world and their mis-
apprehension of themselves. Underlying all is West's bitter conviction that there is no communication in our world. Man shares
nothing with man. If man seeks to address his fellow, whether
through the active pursuit of love or the passive submission to
others, he is destroyed. West's conclusion is that the holy fool will
always be misapprehended and destroyed as long as the values of
the industrial American world prevail. Success, money, power—all
conspire to cast out love, to freeze the heart, to dull sensibility.

Nathanael West's *Miss Lonelyhearts*
Between the Dead Pan and
the Unborn Christ

by *Robert J. Andreach*

Nathanael West's *Miss Lonelyhearts* is finally receiving the careful attention it deserves. In the course of important studies, critics have compared it to the pessimistic literature of our age, with its delineation of the sterile wasteland and the empty American dream, and to the work of writers such as Dostoevsky, Eliot, and the French Surrealists. I would like to extend their findings by relating the novel to the Pan-Christ antagonism, for I believe its unifying principle is the antagonism that pits the virile, sexual, natural paganism against the effeminate, ascetic, materialistic Christianity, a major theme in Western literature from the Romantic period through Poem III of Pound's *Hugh Selwyn Mauberley* and O'Neill's *Great God Brown*.

There is a well-established tradition—found, for example, in Plutarch's *De Oraculorum Defectu*—that when the angels announced the birth of the Christ child, a cry of lamentation came out of the earth, "Great Pan is dead." Students of the Renaissance know the force of this tradition from the arguments of the Christian Humanists, Milton's "Nativity Hymn," and Book I of *Paradise Lost*. But there have always been interesting departures, even be-

"*Nathanael West's* Miss Lonelyhearts *Between the Dead Pan and the Unborn Christ*" *by Robert J. Andreach. From* Modern Fiction Studies *12 (Spring 1966–Winter 1967), 251–60. Copyright © 1969 by the Purdue Research Foundation, Lafayette, Indiana. Reprinted by permission of the Purdue Research Foundation. The editor has omitted three bibliographical footnotes.*

49

fore the Romantic period. To give but one, the Glosse to Maye in Spenser's *Shepheardes Calender* says, "Great pan is Christ, the very God of all shepheards, which calleth himselfe the greate and good shepherd. The name is most rightly (me thinks) applyed to him, for Pan signifieth all or omnipotent, which is only the Lord Jesus." *Miss Lonelyhearts* is a contemporary variation—a brutal, despairing one—which this paper will demonstrate is West's allegory of modern man's predicament.

The goat-god Pan, half animal and half man in appearance with a face distinguished by a sardonic smile, was a pastoral god of fertility in primitive myth and ritual. Forever playing his flute, or reed pipes, and notoriously ugly, he devoted much of his time to licentious revelry, although, like Dionysus, he was a god of pain and suffering, death and rebirth as well. As a result of his name and the fertility rites surrounding him, he came to be the personification of Nature and all of paganism. From the Christian point of view, however, the Pan conception was a satanic carnality. Christianity denounced his cult, but instead of eliminating it only succeeded in driving his worship underground. He was discredited, though, for by the age of medieval drama, Pan, one of the horned gods, became the Devil with horns and cloven feet—both devil and buffoon.

The antagonism is introduced in the three letters Miss Lonelyhearts reads in the opening chapter of the novel. Sick-of-it-all has had seven children in twelve years. Despite her doctor's warnings she is pregnant again and in terrible pain, but her husband refuses to permit an abortion. His belief that Christianity insists she be fecund ruins her sexual pleasure and her health. Desperate is a sixteen-year-old girl who, because she was born without a nose, does not have dates as other girls do. It was not so bad when she was a little girl, for she "got used to the kids on the block making fun of" her. Her father thinks she is "being punished for his sins." Harold's sister Gracie—a play on God's grace—a deaf and dumb girl who has been raped, will be beaten by their parents. Further, "if the boys on the blok hear about it they will say dirty things like they did on Peewee Conors sister the time she got caught in the lots," the modern habitat for kids, the modern worshipers of Pan.

The novel tells of the search for Christ by Miss Lonelyhearts, a writer of an advice-to-the-lovelorn column who is overwhelmed by the misery of those who appeal to him. Shrike, his editor, who is usually drunk and who torments him with his sardonic deflation of man's spiritual needs, is identified in the title of the second chapter as "the dead pan." Joining his columnist in Delehanty's speakeasy, he reveals the cause of his bitterness when he pulls out a newspaper clipping about a " 'goat and adding machine' ritual" for a condemned slayer (p. 73). The religion of the modern world has linked his natural religion with a machine. Powerless to overcome Christianity, his defense is cynicism or the thrust of his horns at Miss Lonelyhearts, the "butt for Shrike's jokes" (p. 89). His sensuality is vividly illustrated in the scene in which he appears in the doorway naked from the waist down (p. 96). More than merely comic, he is meant to be satanic also, for when he embraces Miss Farkis, he buries "his triangular face like the blade of a hatchet in her neck" (p. 74). The triangle is an age-old sexual symbol; the blow on the neck, the mark of the Devil.[1] Later, Goldsmith, one of Shrike's followers, drops his heavy arm on Miss Lonelyhearts' "neck like the arm of a deadfall" (p. 97).

Although not especially successful in his amorous escapades, Pan managed an occasional seduction, the most famous being with Diana, a member of the Artemis-Selene moon goddess constellation. A virgin and a huntress noted for her speed, she was a goddess of the female reproductive principle. At the temple of Artemis at Ephesus, she is represented with a multitude of breasts.

Shrike adores breasts. Describing one of his admirers as being very intelligent, he carves "two enormous breasts in the air with his hands" (p. 72). At his apartment he declares his intention " 'to make a clean breast of matters, a nice clean breast. It's better to make a clean breast of matters than to let them fester in the depths of one's soul' " (p. 92). His wife Mary, Diana's modern counterpart, uses her breasts "as the coquettes of long ago had used

[1] Margaret Alice Murray, *The God of the Witches* (New York, 1952), pp. 99–102.

their fans" (p. 90). Between them she wears a medal commemorating her speed—"first place in the 100 yd. dash"—and by leaning forward just enough so that Miss Lonelyhearts can see the medal, she constantly titillates him.

In Mary's unhappy marriage to Shrike, we have the predicament of modern man in comic miniature. His interest in her is purely sexual and on such an incredibly crude level that he encourages her dating because, as she complains, " 'He knows that I let them neck me and when I get home all hot and bothered, why he climbs into my bed and begs for it. The cheap bastard!' " (p. 93). She will not leave him, however, for she has the Pan principle in her, which he satisfies. She will go dancing with Miss Lonelyhearts, but by not sleeping with him, she refuses "to give Shrike horns" (p. 89), make him a cuckold. That is, she cannot give her entire being to Pan: " 'She was a virgin when I married her and has been fighting ever since to remain one' " (p. 92). Nor can she invest her instincts with a sacramental quality; instead she dreams of escaping to gaiety, which turns out to be the fraudulent El Gaucho night club. Since her dream is never fulfilled, she always returns to her husband's bed, but she cannot enjoy uninhibited sensuality either. The one time Shrike shows pain occurs when he summarizes their relationship: " 'Sleeping with her is like sleeping with a knife in one's groin' " (p. 92).

All of the other characters, excluding Betty at the beginning of the novel, are part-Pan: the clean old man has a voice "like a flute" and the cough of a goat; Broad Shoulders' husband's face is "like the mask of a devil," the sight of whom temporarily paralyzed her from the "waist down"; the woman with rheum in her eyes "wears heavy boots on her torn and bleeding feet"; the boy with the violin is a "kid." They are inhibited worshipers because they cannot reconcile their Pan instincts and their consciousness that these instincts are sinful. On the one hand, the men in the speakeasy reminisce about initiation ceremonies, gang rapes; on the other hand, they have their pathetic dreams of spiritual relief. There is no community infused with a life that will explain their desires and suffering and of which they can be members. As one of them says about the possibility of a genuine religious experience, " 'It would be personal and so meaningless, except to a psychologist' " (p. 83).

West's handling of the allegory is masterful. The novel reproduces both in society and in man what happened historically: Christianity sought to extirpate the Pan cult but only drove it underground, to reappear clandestinely in disguised form. Shrike is reduced to meeting his quasi-followers daily in the speakeasy, located "in the cellar of a brownstone house" (p. 71), where violence keeps erupting. He cannot regain his throne because he is the sole Pan in a Christian society and hence dead as a deity. He cannot even command the undivided allegiance of his wife. As Christians the characters want to deny their Pan impulses, but since they are merely subterranean, they keep erupting also. For West this conflict between body and soul, instincts and conscience, causes schizophrenia.

The schizophrenia is best seen in the protagonist. He is a "New England puritan" with a goat-like face: "His forehead was high and narrow. His nose was long and fleshless. His bony chin was shaped and cleft like a hoof" (p. 69). While searching for Christ he plays with Betty's breasts, tries "to excite himself into eagerness by thinking of the play Mary made with her breasts" (p. 90), and eventually kisses them. Unlike the others, his predicament is tragic, for, unlike the others, he has the Christ dream to an acute degree. "If he could only believe in Christ, then adultery would be a sin, then everything would be simple and the letters extremely easy to answer" (p. 99).

What makes his predicament hopeless is that belief in Christ is no solution since for West Christ was never born, and whenever Miss Lonelyhearts attempts to make Him a reality, he invariably brings back to life the dead Pan, the world of primitive sensuality that lies waiting within him. When he chants, " 'Christ, Christ,' " the "snake started to uncoil in his brain." Calling upon Christ unleashes "hysteria, a snake whose scales are tiny mirrors in which the dead world takes on a semblance of life" (pp. 75–76). In his tortured dream in Chapter III, he relives a savage ritual which took place after an argument about the existence of God while he was at college. "It was spring. The sun and the smell of vegetable birth renewed their drunkenness and they reeled between the loaded carts." Singing "an obscene version of 'Mary Had a Little Lamb,'" he and two companions set out to sacrifice a lamb to God. The scene ends in "frenzy" and "slimy blood" as Miss Lonelyhearts, the "elected priest," crushes the lamb's head after twice failing with his knife. The columnist cannot fuse his pre-Christian impulses and his Christian conscience. In the telephone booth before meeting Mrs. Doyle, he fastens "his eyes on two disembodied genitals" (p. 99). Later, in his imagination he constructs a phallus and then a cross (p. 105).

In the park he walks "into the shadow of a lamp-post that lay on the path like a spear. It pierced him like a spear" (p. 70), both the spear that pierced Christ and the lance, which, with the cup, are "sex symbols of immemorial antiquity and worldwide diffusion, the Lance, or Spear, representing the Male, the Cup, or Vase, the Female, reproductive energy." [2] Hermes, Pan's father, was a phallic god, and the stones that formed the basis of his worship were phallic symbols,[3] as they are in the novel. Shrike suggests that Miss Lonelyhearts recommend stones to distraught letter writers: " 'Teach them to pray each morning: "Give us this day our daily stone." ' " The protagonist has given all of his way away except one, and it is this one periodic urge that he cannot control, that "had formed in his gut" (p. 71). Note that in the dream sequence he crushes the lamb's head with a stone. In conflict with his conscience, it drives him to his tragedy. In a passage not far removed in meaning from "The Dynamo and the Virgin" chapter of *The Education of Henry Adams,* he universalizes his tragedy into The American one: "Americans have dissipated their racial energy in an orgy of stone breaking. In their few years they have broken more stones than did centuries of Egyptians. And they have done their work hysterically, desperately, almost as if they knew that the stones would some day break them" (p. 100).

The tension generated by his flesh-spirit dichotomy overpowers him with chaos. Needing order, he turns to Betty, who "when she

[2] Jessie L. Weston, *From Ritual to Romance* (New York, 1957), p. 75.
[3] Robert Graves, *The Greek Myths,* 2 vols. (New York, 1957), I, 56, n. 1 and 102, n. 2.

straightened his tie, she straightened much more" (p. 79). Betty represents a third level of existence: the world of unconscious nature. But she can never provide him with salvation precisely because she is unconscious and he is not. Once awakened to the spiritual needs of a Christian, he can never regress to her level, just as he can never become a Pan enthusiast again. She is unconscious of spiritual suffering: "Her world was not the world and could never include the readers of his column" (p. 79). When he tries to tell her that quitting his job will not alter his predicament, he sadly realizes that she cannot understand him. In her Edenic innocence she believes that communion with nature will cure him.

Then, too, Betty's unconsciousness brings out the Pan in him. By the time he reaches her, his "panic," the dread that the non-disciple of Pan experiences when he wanders into the goat-god's domain, "had turned to irritation" (p. 79). Her passivity, however, stirs his tendency to violence. When he gets angry at her, "she raised her arm as though to ward off a blow" (p. 81). She will be his sacrificial victim, triggering his sensuality into action.

The one way he can bring to life the unborn Christ is through violence, but by resorting to it, he releases the Pan presence which lurks beneath the surface of his self-sacrifice. Earlier we saw what happened when he chanted, "Christ," and what happened when he offered the lamb to God. Initially he wants to console the clean old man, but the longer he talks to him, the more he becomes enraged until he commences to twist his arm: "He was twisting the arm of all the sick and miserable, broken and betrayed, inarticulate and impotent. He was twisting the arm of Desperate, Broken-hearted, Sick-of-it-all, Disillusioned-with-tubercular-husband" (p. 88).

After his failure with Mary Shrike, who, in spite of his kissing her breasts, leaves him for her husband, Miss Lonelyhearts goes to Fay Doyle, a massive sea spirit with "breasts like balloons" (p. 100) who makes "sea sounds" while undressing. "Her call for him to hurry was a sea-moan, and when he lay beside her, she heaved, tidal, moon-driven" (p. 101). Since the moon was regarded as the source of all water, she is related to the moon goddess constellation. Mrs. Doyle is the most uninhibited female in the novel. She seduces him; on his second visit to her apartment, she attempts to arouse him sexually; she even tries "to force his head between her breasts" (p. 130). From her point of view Christian charity or any form of self-sacrifice is a perversion, for she calls her husband and Miss Lonelyhearts " 'fairies' " for holding hands (p. 129).

Immersion in fertility provides no lessening of his burden either. Mrs. Doyle intensifies his suffering because as an immense figure of life she communicates "a gigantic, living Miss Lonelyhearts letter" of misery. The more life one encounters, the more suffering one experiences. He crawls out of bed "exhausted"; when she desires him again she has to "drag" him back to bed (pp. 101–104).

This brings us to the central, and most pessimistic, chapter of the novel. Miss Lonelyhearts knows that Betty cannot aid him. Unconscious, she cannot understand his spiritual agony; she can minister to his body only. Nonetheless he allows himself to follow her plan to partake of the curative powers of pristine nature on the Connecticut farm. He seems to improve until he approaches her sexually. Since she is a virgin, she does not respond, and he respectfully ceases. The next morning he observes that "although spring was well advanced, in the deep shade there was nothing but death—rotten leaves, gray and white fungi, and over everything a funereal hush." That same day he, naked, sits watching her, naked, hang clothes. The remainder of the chapter must be quoted:

> Somewhere in the woods a thrush was singing. Its sound was like that of a flute choked with saliva.
> Betty stopped with her arms high to listen to the bird. When it was quiet, she turned towards him with a guilty laugh. He blew her a kiss. She caught it with a gesture that was childishly sexual. He vaulted the porch rail and ran to kiss her. As they went down, he smelled a mixture of sweat, soap and crushed grass (p. 114).

The bird's sound is the call of Pan. As soon as she awakens to it, and her sexual nature, she feels "guilty." In order to comprehend her guilt, we have to return to the second chapter, where Shrike designates the "bird" that the non-pagan hunts as the soul. The singing of the bird awakens Betty to her natural sexual desires at the same time that it awakens her to her Christian consciousness.

For the first time she feels "guilty." She now has the predicament of the other characters. She will not be able to reconcile her pagan impulses with her Christian conscience. As the last line makes absolutely clear, she and he fall from her Eden.

Rather than being rescued by her, Miss Lonelyhearts corrupts her innocence, for she will never be able to return to unconsciousness. She, too, will find neither escape nor salvation. In Chapter VIII ("Dismal Swamp"), before the trip to the country, she left his room as soon as Shrike entered, whereas in Chapter XIII ("Attends a Party"), after the trip, she is one of the guests at Shrike's party; she bursts out crying in the drugstore; she is willing to have an abortion; and in what is the most illuminating symbol in the novel, she agrees to marry him and fragmentize their life together: "With a great deal of laughter, they decided to have three beds in thir bedroom. Twin beds for sleep, very prim and puritanical, and between them a love bed, an ornate double bed with cupids, nymphs and Pans" (p. 138).

Determined to know Christ, Miss Lonelyhearts leaves his bed, in which he has sought escape from the consuming nightmare of suffering, to acquire humility and to preach the Word—to fail "still more miserably" because at the mention of "Christ," he gets "hysterical" (p. 129). Following his fruitless attempts to find spiritual relief with Mary, Mrs. Doyle, and Betty and to give spiritual relief to Doyle, he becomes rock-like, insensitive to all, including Betty's tears. "He did not feel guilty. He did not feel. The rock was a solidification of his feeling, his conscience, his sense of reality, his self-knowledge" (p. 138). His denial of his nature is an invitation to madness. Betty asks him as he stands smiling in the midst of Shrike's revelers, " 'What's the matter with you? . . . Are you sick again?' " (p. 133). He is sick, for he "climbs aboard his bed again" to welcome the "arrival of fever" (p. 138) and his insane religious experience.

Miss Lonelyhearts believes that his one means of imitating Christ's sacrifice of His godhead to assume human nature is by a shattering of his nature. If he can accomplish this agonizing self-sacrifice, he will be moving toward the true Christian's goal. Christianity will therefore be a living religion for him, and he

will be on the way of salvation. At the same time he knows that
any act of violence really resurrects the submerged Pan instincts.
By killing his feelings, he hopes to avert what took place with
the lamb and the clean old man. If possible, it is so only at the
cost of his sanity, and it is also possible that the inevitable happens
anyway. In the light of his climbing into bed as Shrike does and
Doyle's ripping his fly open when he tries to practice Christian
charity and his staring at the Christ on the wall until it becomes
"a bright fly," we suspect he is bringing to life the phallic Pan.
He does not realize it, though. In his madness he sees himself as
a Christ-like figure whom "God had sent . . . [to] perform a miracle," and he rushes out to embrace Doyle.

The focus of attention in the last two paragraphs of the novel
shifts to Peter Doyle, crippled both physically and spiritually, who
has come for revenge because of the columnist's affair with his
wife. In the middle of the stairway Doyle "turns to escape" from
the imposition, from above, of Miss Lonelyhearts' insane Christ
complex. While they are struggling Betty enters, below, and "cuts
off his escape." Doyle is trapped between a dream that when put
into reality becomes perverted and a once unconscious nature now
corrupted.

We have seen how West utilizes symbols with two levels of meaning: the spear symbolizes phallic worship and Christ's Passion. We
may have the same possibility in this paragraph. If Doyle's "gun"
that "explodes" accidentally is a phallic symbol, it means that the
protagonist's violence does for Doyle exactly what it did for him;
it activates his Pan nature. Ironically, the man who set out to be
a Christian redeemer ends up a primitive victim. If the "gun" is
simply a mechanical weapon, it means that the same materialism
that converted Pan's cult into a " 'goat and adding machine' ritual"
ironically kills Miss Lonelyhearts in his spiritual quest. Of course,
it may mean both. In any case, they "roll part of the way down
the stairs." Doyle is caught between an unborn higher religion and
a dead religion. He stops between a dream that can only be perverted if pursued and a reality that was once innocent and natural.
There is one final turn of the screw. For all of Miss Lonelyhearts'
idealism while alive, now that he is dead his body "drags the
cripple" down toward Betty.

For West there is no solution to the Christian's predicament. Christianity forces man's pagan instincts underground yet fails to supply him with anything that will transmute the basic facts of existence, suffering and desire, into a means to salvation. Christ's Incarnation, Passion, and Redemption would do that—the fertility cult symbols could be made to serve His end—but He was never born. The truth most noticeably lacking in West's world is God's grace, which operates toward transforming nature and assisting man in his spiritual growth. Miss Lonelyhearts is in despair because he cannot find Him. He is a dream, not a reality, and if one persists in the Christ dream to its conclusion, he perverts it by reawakening his animal nature. For West all that Christianity does for man is give him a consciousness of a higher reality, which prevents him from remaining unconscious, and a conscience, which prevents him from enjoying his sexual nature without feeling guilty. The paradox which destroys Miss Lonelyhearts is that it takes violence for him to bring Christ to life but violence is just what Christianity banished, and when he allows himself to become violent, he becomes the priest and the victim of an ancient and bloody ritual.

Because Pan can be resurrected only through the violation of one's conscience and Christ can be born only through the violation of one's nature, modern man lives in a wasteland: "As far as he could discover, there were no signs of spring. The decay that covered the surface of the mottled ground was not the kind in which life generates. Last year, he remembered, May had failed to quicken these soiled fields. It had taken all the brutality of July to torture a few green spikes through the exhausted dirt" (p. 70). The person who wants to revivify himself and the sterile land is in a dilemma. He faces two disastrous alternatives. He can kill his conscience and become a dead Pan in a Christian society, or he can kill his nature and become a madman, awakening his Pan nature anyway. Without Christ to show the way, he is in an impasse.[4]

---

[4] Comparing Dostoevsky and West, Arthur Cohen, "Nathanael West's Holy Fool," *Commonweal*, LXIV (June 15, 1956), 276–278, writes that the latter "on the contrary, anticipates nothing that is to come. It is his merit to have described with unbelieveable clarity the destruction that has passed, the pestilence that has visited us and has been invited to stay."

There is no hope of spiritual rebirth, despite Elizabeth Barrett Browning's "The Dead Pan," which contains the following:

> Look up, poets, to the sun!
> Pan, Pan is dead.
> Christ hath sent us down the angels;
> And the whole earth and the skies
> Are illumed by altar-candles
> Lit for blessed mysteries;
> And a Priest's hand through creation
> Waveth calm and consecration.
> And Pan is dead.

Since Bulfinch quotes two stanzas from her poem (including the line, "Look up, poets, to the sun!") in the section on Pan in his *Mythology,* to which West refers in his notes on the novel,[5] we can read the following passage as his pessimistic answer: "He searched the sky for a target. But the gray sky looked as if it had been rubbed with a soiled eraser. It held no angels, flaming crosses, olive-bearing doves, wheels within wheels. Only a newspaper struggled in the air like a kite with a broken spine" (p. 71).

West gives his final poignant and chilling word in *The Day of the Locust.* Listening to Bach's "Come Redeemer, Our Saviour," Tod Hackett notes the changes in the tone. When the music begs, "Now come, O our Saviour," he muses, "If there was a hint of a threat, . . . just a hint, and a tiny bit of impatience, could Bach be blamed? After all, when he wrote this music, the world had already been waiting for its lover more than seventeen hundred years. . . . Perhaps Christ heard. If He did, He gave no sign" (p. 349). So long as Gracie remains deaf, dumb, and raped on the roof of the apartment house, the men and women in the apartment house have no hope.

[5] "Some Notes on *Miss Lonelyhearts*," *Contempo,* III (May 15, 1933), 1-2.

To Kill God and Build a Church:
Nathanael West's *Miss Lonelyhearts*

by *Robert I. Edenbaum*

In 1932, the year before *Miss Lonelyhearts* was published, Nathanael West published early versions of several chapters of his book in little magazines. Though much of the material eventually appeared in the final version (April 1933), there are important differences in the drafts themselves and between them and the completed book. In the February 1932 issue of *Contact* West used the third person, in the May issue the first person, in October the third again. In February Miss Lonelyhearts has a name, Thomas Matlock; in all later versions he is only "Miss Lonelyhearts." Shrike was apparently conceived early in the progress of the book, for the name appears in the earliest installment, but dialogue and interior monologue given to Miss Lonelyhearts in the drafts were only later transferred to Shrike. The conception of Miss Lonelyhearts himself underwent significant changes; lines were transferred without change or with slight alterations from Miss Lonelyhearts to Shrike—the following, for example: "The Susan Chesters, the Beatrice Fairfaxs [sic], the Miss Lonelyhearts are the priests of twentieth century America"; ". . . don't embarrass oneself and them [the letter-writers] with love. Don't like lepers" (February 1932). Material from the first-person draft was omitted entirely: ". . . don't misunderstand me. My Christ has nothing to do with love. Even before I became Miss Lonelyhearts, my world was moribund. I lived on a deserted stairway, among steel engravings of or-

"To Kill God and Build a Church: Nathanael West's Miss Lonelyhearts*" by Robert I. Edenbaum. From* The CEA Critic *29 (June, 1967) 5–7, and 11. Reprinted by permission of the author and the publisher.*

nate machinery. I wrote my first love letters on a typewriter. . . .
I turned to Christ as the most familiar and natural of excitants. I
wanted him to destroy this hypnosis. He alone could make the
rock of sensation bleed and the stick of thought flower" (May 1932).
In the magazine version of "Miss Lonelyhearts and the clean old
man," the old man "turned away to wipe himself"; in the book
he is sitting on the closed seat of the toilet.

In the July *Contempo* the entire speech demolishing alternatives
of escape (the South Seas, the arts, the farm), later given to Shrike,
is Miss Lonelyhearts' stream of consciousness. Each paragraph is a
long, unpunctuated Joycean sentence. The piece is introduced with
a squib omitted from the book: "The Miss Lonelyhearts of the
New York Evening Hawk . . . sits staring through his office window into the street . . . Although the street is walled at both
ends, he has a Bible in one hand and a philosophy book in the
other. In his lap are travel, art, seed and gun catalogues."
The omissions and changes indicate the transition from the im-
mature *The Dream Life of Balso Snell* to the maturity of *Miss
Lonelyhearts*. In the final version the jokes are all given to Shrike
and his imitators; in the earlier versions the jokes are at times Miss
Lonelyhearts', and more important, West's. The "clever" subordination of the sentence "Although the street is walled at both
ends, he has a Bible in one hand . . ." could easily appear in
Balso Snell; it has no place in *Miss Lonelyhearts*. It is at the same
time too cryptic and too obvious. "I wrote my first love letter on
a typewriter," too, might be Balso's line, but not Miss Lonelyhearts'.
It makes much more sense for the cynical Shrike to call Miss Lonelyhearts "a leper-licker" than for Miss Lonelyhearts to call himself
that. The elimination of the pointlessly indelicate detail of the old
man wiping himself speaks for itself. Even the change of the name
of the newspaper from the Evening Hawk to the Post-Dispatch is
significant, for it indicates that West realized that he had to create
an acceptable world, not a comic-book fantasy.
The differences between versions indicate not only that West's
conception of his characters changed and coalesced, but that he
gradually came to take himself, his writing, and the world more

seriously. It would perhaps not be overstating the case to say that West underwent a transformation similar to that which he credits to his hero: "A man is hired to give advice to the readers of a newspaper. The job is a circulation stunt and the whole staff considers it a joke . . . He too considers the job a joke, but after several months at it, the joke begins to escape him. . . . For the first time in his life, he is forced to examine the values by which he lives. This examination shows him that he is the victim of the joke and not its perpetrator." [p. 106] I am not hypothesizing about changes in West's psyche, but suggesting that *Miss Lonelyhearts* started out much closer to the cruel shenanigans of *Balso Snell* than it finished. The difference between the two books is measurable in terms of the letter-writers; their letters bring a very real world, and a very real evil, lacking in *Balso Snell,* into *Miss Lonelyhearts.*

Dear Miss Lonelyhearts—

I am sixteen years old and I dont know what to do and would appreciate it if you could tell me what to do. When I was a little girl it was not so bad because I got used to the kids on the block making fun of me, but now I would like to have boy friends like the other girls and go out on Saturday nites, but no boy will take me because I was born without a nose—although I am a good dancer and have a nice shape and my father buys me pretty clothes. . . . What did I do to deserve such a terrible bad fate? Even if I did do some bad things I didnt do any before I was a year old and I was born this way. I asked Papa and he says he doesnt know, but that maybe I did something in the other world before I was born or that maybe I was being punished for his sins. I dont believe that because he is a very nice man. Ought I commit suicide?

Sincerely yours,

Desperate (p. 67)

West still calculates his shocks; he holds back the fact of the girl's nose until a subordinate clause toward the end of a long, rambling sentence, then redoubles the shock with an anticlimatic false subordination that is almost more terrible than the missing nose itself—"although I am a good dancer and have a nice shape. . . ." He makes laughter doubly impossible by the pathetic gentleness and politeness of the letter—of, for example, *"Ought*

I commit suicide?" instead of "should I." The misspellings and poor grammar are not funny, for the common denominator in the letters is an innocence that makes the fact of their having been written to Miss Lonelyhearts an unlaughable irony: Miss Lonelyhearts may be a holy fool, but he is considerably less innocent than his correspondents.

In another letter: "I was married honorable from our church but I never knew what married life meant as I never was told about man and wife. My grandmother never told me and she was the only mother I had but made a big mistake by not telling me as it dont pay to be innocent and [it] is only a big disapointment" (p. 66). At the end of this passage "it" is first used generally, while the "it" that is omitted from the parallel (added in square brackets) refers to sexual experience; the meaning shifts away from innocence to the fruit of innocence, the emptiness of sex in the life of the letter-writer.

This is the world that is "no longer funny" to Miss Lonelyhearts. Not a word of the letters that appear in the early drafts was changed in the final version of the book: one can speculate that the letters forced West to carefully distinguish between Shrike's dialogue and thought process and Miss Lonelyhearts'; forced him, that is, to define and clarify his characters, and, perhaps, his own mind.

If Miss Lonelyhearts submerges the world in his own ego, the letter-writers, nevertheless, are a constant which constitutes a very real world. A note on contributors in *Contempo* described *Balso Snell* as a "satiric farce" and *Miss Lonelyhearts* as a "moral satire." The letters themselves are the measure of the difference between those two terms; despite the mad point of view in *Miss Lonelyhearts,* the letters bring the concrete and omnipresent fact of evil into the novel and mark West's development away from the inversion of *Balso Snell*. His major theme from *Miss Lonelyhearts* on, in Isaac Rosenfeld's words, is "the secret inner life of the masses," their search for a usable dream, and the corruption of dreams by the mass media. The heart, circle, swastika, cross, and the other symbols that Miss Lonelyhearts tries to form in one of his dreams, all represent attempts—though certainly not identical ones—at dreams to serve as weapons in a battle for order, which is synonymous with the search for a reality.

Early in the novel Miss Lonelyhearts searches the sky for a sign, a "target," but "It held no angels, flaming crosses, olive-bearing doves, wheels within wheels. Only a newspaper struggled in the air like a kite with a broken spine" (p. 71). The newspaper replaces Ezekiel's wheels within wheels. Shrike, no less than Miss Lonelyhearts, is aware of the existence of the letters, but he is cynically willing to accept the substitution; he "advises" Miss Lonelyhearts on the way to run his column: ". . . give your readers stones. When they ask for bread don't give them crackers as does the Church and don't, like the State, tell them to eat cake. Explain that man cannot live by bread alone and give them stones. Tell them to pray each morning: 'Give us this day our daily stone'" (pp. 70–71). Miss Lonelyhearts' mental response to this is that "He had given his readers many stones; so many, in fact, that he had only one left—the stone that had formed in his gut. . . . If he could only throw the stone. He searched the sky for a target" (p. 71). In his metaphysical rebellion, Miss Lonelyhearts' aim, finally, is to kill God. The identification of the newspaper itself as the purveyor of false dreams, in place of symbols of order once more potent, is made explicit when Miss Lonelyhearts returns from his futile attempt to escape from the letters to the idyll of country life; on his return to the city, he sees only misery around him—"a man who appeared to be on the verge of death stagger[s] into a movie theater that was showing a picture called *Blonde Beauty* . . . a ragged woman with an enormous goiter pick[s] a love story magazine out of a garbage can and seem[s] very excited by her find" (p. 115). He generalizes on these incidents: "Men have always fought their misery with dreams. Although dreams were once powerful, they have been made puerile by the movies, radio, and newspapers. Among many betrayals, this one is the worst" (p. 115).

Shrike's answer to the betrayal is to crack jokes. Betty's is to live as though the letter-writers do not exist, "to limit experience arbitrarily." Miss Lonelyhearts sees that "Her world was not the world and could never include the readers of his column" (p. 79), and he rejects her method when he decides that "his confusion was sig-

nificant, while her order was not" (p. 79). There are moments when
Miss Lonelyhearts fools himself into thinking that he has found
a workable solution, but they are short-lived. He decides he has
fooled himself in thinking that marriage to Betty is a way out.
He plays with the "snake" of hysteria, luring it out of himself,
then stopping, afraid of it. When it does break out, it is neither
completely uncontrolled nor completely unpremeditated. "Only
violence could make him mobile," but his own explosion into violence only increases his guilt.

If Miss Lonelyhearts' own perceptions do not demolish the possibility of escape, Shrike, the butcher bird, is there to remind him
that there is no escape. Shrike offers, then devastates, the possibility
of escape to the soil, the South Seas, escape through hedonism,
art, suicide, drugs. Shrike agrees that God is the only escape, but
his church is "the First Church of Christ Dentist, where He is
worshiped as Preventer of Decay" (p. 110).

West ties together his image of the world as a chaos of discon-
nected objects and the theme of the betrayal of the dreams of the
masses by making the objects themselves part of "the business of
dreams," for they are "the paraphernalia of suffering." At one point
in the novel, Miss Lonelyhearts, in an attempt to find "a clue to
his own exhaustion," examines the skyscrapers surrounding a little
park and discovers what he takes to be a possible explanation of
his dilemma: "Americans have dissipated their racial energy in an
orgy of stone breaking. In their few years they have broken more
stones than did centuries of Egyptians. And they have done their
work hysterically, desperately, almost as if they knew that the stones
would someday break them" (p. 100). In a mechanized world, the
energy that once went into the old, lost symbols goes into the manu-
facture and worship of objects themselves instead of into the ordering of them into some sort of meaningful whole; the objects usurp
the function of some ordering principle beyond them. Instead of
working towards reality, America fragments it and substitutes the
fantasies offered by the movies, newspapers, and radio—the same
dreams that Shrike shows to be unrealizable. The tragedy of the
girl born without a nose is not only that she is deformed but that
she dreams of a handsome boy friend to take her out on Saturday

nights. If Miss Lonelyhearts cannot take the dreams seriously, neither can he refuse to take the people themselves seriously.

The only solution Miss Lonelyhearts thinks possible, the only dream he is capable of dreaming, is the "Christ-dream." But that too fails when he tries to use it as a weapon against chaos, as a proffered salvation to a world of suffering which he cannot ignore; when he offers his own Christ-dream to Mr. and Mrs. Doyle, he can give them only the platitudes of his column or the rhetoric of Shrike. All that remains is his ego; the only reality is inside himself—the stone "in his gut." The only real world is the world within, which contains and distorts the external world.

At the end of the chapter "Miss Lonelyhearts and the clean old man," the earlier statement that "only violence could make him mobile" is borne out for the first time when Miss Lonelyhearts insists that the old man tell his life story (for the same reason that, later, he reads a bulky letter from one of his correspondents: "for the same reason that an animal tears at a wounded foot: to hurt the pain"). Where, in *The Day of the Locust*, Tod Hackett is "galvanized into activity"—his painting—by violence, Miss Lonelyhearts moves closer, by means of violence, to his consummating transformation. He twists the old man's arm until someone hits him on the head with a chair. At the beginning of the next chapter Miss Lonelyhearts wakes up in his bed: "His head ached and his thoughts revolved inside the pain like a wheel within a wheel. When he opened his eyes, the room, like a third wheel, revolved around the pain in his head" (p. 88). He approaches his union with Christ, the center of the wheels within wheels which, earlier, he had looked for in vain in the sky. It is not in the sky, but within him.

In the calm just previous to his complete "apotheosis," Miss Lonelyhearts *becomes* a rock as West, using one of his favorite devices, starts with a simile, then allows it to take over literally. Miss Lonelyhearts becomes impervious to the world like "an ancient rock, smooth with experience" (p. 132). Then West pushes home the image violently, for he does not intend his imagery to be at all subtle: "The rock remained calm and solid" (p. 132); "what goes on in the sea is of no interest to the rock" (p. 134); when Miss Lonelyhearts realizes that Betty dresses for occasions, "Even the rock was touched by this realization. No; it was not the rock that was touched. The rock was still perfect. It was his mind that was touched, the instrument with which he knew the rock" (p. 136). Finally, in the last chapter, "After a long night and morning, towards noon, Miss Lonelyhearts welcomed the arrival of fever. It promised heat and mentally unmotivated violence. The promise was soon fulfilled; the rock became a furnace" (p. 138). The ego becomes all the world there is; the only "real" is the surreal. Miss Lonelyhearts finds his way to the wheels within wheels, but at the price of dementia and death.

At least one critic states that Miss Lonelyhearts tries to find the true Christ, and gains a mystical union with God only to be misunderstood by the world. It would be more reasonable, however, to apply to Miss Lonelyhearts the aim Albert Camus attributes to man in revolt: "To kill God and to build a Church." Camus writes, further,

> The protest against evil which is at the very core of metaphysical revolt . . . [lies] in the fact that the suffering is not justified . . . In the eyes of the rebel, what is missing from the misery of the world, as well as from its moments of happiness, is some principle by which they can be explained. The insurrection against evil is, above all, a demand for unity. The rebel obstinately confronts a world condemned to death and the impenetrable obscurity of the human condition with his demand for life and absolute religion. Rebellion, even though it is blind, is a form of asceticism. Therefore, if the rebel blasphemes, it is in the hope of finding a new god. He staggers under the shock of the first and most profound of all religious experiences. It is not rebellion itself that is noble, but its aim, even though its achievements are at times ignoble.[1]

Certainly Miss Lonelyhearts is searching for a religion, but to suggest that his dementia is a usable solution is ludicrous. His symbolic metamorphosis into a rock at the end of the novel when he becomes his own Church (in what is probably West's intentional pun) hardly represents the triumph of faith and love. To claim

---

[1] Albert Camus, *The Rebel* (New York, 1960), p. 101.

that Miss Lonelyhearts' demand for unity and clarity is satisfied is to be as repelled by West's pessimism as are his most severe detractors.

As Camus suggests about much of the metaphysical rebellion of the last hundred and fifty years, Miss Lonelyhearts' aims rather than his achievements are "noble." The deadness and disorder of his surreal world, and his own despair, lead only to frustration and consequent violence—against the clean old man, Mrs. Doyle, Mary Shrike, Betty. He twists the old man's arm—which becomes the arm of all the letter-writers—because the old man (and the letter-writers) are living proof that he is not the Messiah, that salvation is not at hand. In that sense the existence of the letter-writers is a continual affront to Miss Lonelyhearts. At his death—assuming that the exploding gun does kill him—he leaves Betty pregnant and perhaps teaches even her that her arbitrary narrowing of experience is a lie. That is the exent of his achievement, that and a twentieth century version of a mystical experience.

But Miss Lonelyhearts' aim—and West's—is not ignoble. If Miss Lonelyhearts' approach is not usable, still less so is Betty's or Shrike's. It is impossible to ignore or to laugh at the letter-writers; that is as much West's discovery as Miss Lonelyhearts'. West can still use something of the method of the surrealists in *Miss Lonelyhearts*, and their view of the physical world, but he has added the dreams of the letter-writers, has added, not an anonymous mass or mob, but people. Camus, again, writes that the "irrational terror" of the modern world, the surrealists' no less than Hitler's, "transforms men into objects, 'planetary bacilli.' " In *Miss Lonelyhearts* West refuses to treat people as objects as much as he refuses to treat their dreams as jokes. If he despised or pitied them, there is no reason for him to have bothered to create the very real world —if a world viewed from a limited perspective—of *Miss Lonelyhearts*.

Nathanael West

by Stanley Edgar Hyman

Far and away the best of West's books, and in my opinion the only one assured of permanent survival, is *Miss Lonelyhearts*. No one who read West's first book, *The Dream Life of Balso Snell*, a juvenile and somewhat tiresome production, in 1931, could have expected the assured mastery of *Miss Lonelyhearts* two years later, in 1933. In an interview at the time West told A. J. Liebling that it was entirely unlike *Balso Snell*, "of quite a different make, wholesome, clean, holy, slightly mystic and inane." He describes it in an article "Some Notes on Miss Lonelyhearts," as a "portrait of a priest of our time who has had a religious experience." In it, West explains, "violent images are used to illustrate commonplace events. Violent acts are left almost bald." He credits William James's *Varieties of Religious Experience* for its psychology. Some or all of this may be Westian leg-pull.

The plot of *Miss Lonelyhearts* is Sophoclean irony, as simple and inevitable as the plot of *Balso Snell* is random and whimsical. A young newspaperman who writes the agony column of his paper as "Miss Lonelyhearts" has reached the point where the joke has gone sour. He becomes obsessed with the real misery of his correspondents, illuminated for him by the cynicism of William Shrike, the feature editor. Miss Lonelyhearts pursues Shrike's wife Mary, unsuccessfully, and cannot content himself with the love and radiant goodness of Betty, his fiancée. Eventually he finds his fate in

"Nathanael West." From Nathanael West *by Stanley Edgar Hyman (Minneapolis, Minn.: University of Minnesota Press [University of Minnesota Pamphlets on American Writers, No. 21], 1962), pp. 16–29. Copyright © 1962 by the University of Minnesota. Reprinted by permission of the publisher.*

two of his correspondents, the crippled Peter Doyle and his wife Fay. Miss Lonelyhearts is not punished for his tumble with Fay, but when on his next encounter he fights her off, it leads to his being shot by Doyle.

The characters are allegorical figures who are at the same time convincing as people. Miss Lonelyhearts is a New England puritan, the son of a Baptist minister. He has a true religious vocation or calling, but no institutional church to embody it. When Betty suggests that he quit the column, he tells her: "I can't quit. And even if I were to quit, it wouldn't make any difference. I wouldn't be able to forget the letters, no matter what I did."

In one of the most brilliant strokes in the book, he is never named, always identified only by his role. (In an earlier draft, West had named him Thomas Matlock, which we could translate "Doubter Wrestler," but no name at all is infinitely more effective.) Even when he telephones Fay Doyle for an assignation, he identifies himself only as "Miss Lonelyhearts, the man who does the column." In his namelessness, in his vocation without a church, Miss Lonelyhearts is clearly the prophet in the reluctance stage, when he denies the call and tells God that he stammers, but Miss Lonelyhearts, the prophet of *our* time, is stuck there until death.

Miss Lonelyhearts identifies Betty as the principle of order: "She had often made him feel that when she straightened his tie, she straightened much more." The order that she represents is the innocent order of Nature, as opposed to the disorder of sinful Man. When Miss Lonelyhearts is sick, Betty comes to nourish him with hot soup, impose order on his room, and redeem him with a pastoral vision: "She told him about her childhood on a farm and of her love for animals, about country sounds and country smells and of how fresh and clean everything in the country is. She said that he ought to live there and that if he did, he would find that all his troubles were city troubles." When Miss Lonelyhearts is back on his feet, Betty takes him for a walk in the zoo, and he is "amused by her evident belief in the curative power of animals." Then she takes him to live in the country for a few days, in the book's great idyllic scene. Miss Lonelyhearts is beyond help, but it is Betty's patient innocence—she is as soft and helpless

as a kitten—that makes the book so heartbreaking. She is an innocent Eve to his fallen Adam, and he alone is driven out of Eden.

The book's four other principal characters are savage caricatures,
in the root sense of "caricature" as the overloading of one attribute.
Shrike is a dissociated half of Miss Lonelyhearts, his cynical intelligence, and it is interesting to learn that Shrike's rhetorical
masterpiece, the great speech on the varieties of escape, was spoken
by Miss Lonelyhearts in an earlier draft. Shrike's name is marvel-
ously apt. The shrike or butcherbird impales its prey on thorns,
and the name is a form of the word "shriek." Shrike is of course the
mocker who hands Miss Lonelyhearts his crown of thorns, and
throughout the book he is a shrieking bird of prey; when not a
butcherbird, "a screaming, clumsy gull."

Shrike's wife Mary is one vast teasing mammary image. As Miss
Lonelyhearts decides to telephone Mary in Delehanty's speakeasy,
he sees a White Rock poster and observes that "the artist had taken
a great deal of care in drawing her breasts and their nipples stuck
out like tiny red hats." He then thinks of "the play Mary made
with her breasts. She used them as the coquettes of long ago had
used their fans. One of her tricks was to wear a medal low down
on her chest. Whenever he asked to see it, instead of drawing it
out she leaned over for him to look. Although he had often asked
to see the medal, he had not yet found out what it represented."
Miss Lonelyhearts and Mary go out for a gay evening, and Mary
flaunts her breasts while talking of her mother's terrible death from
cancer of the breast. He finally gets to see the medal, which reads
"Awarded by the Boston Latin School for first place in the 100 yd.
dash." When he takes her home he kisses her breasts, for the first
time briefly slowing down her dash.

The Doyles are presented in inhuman or subhuman imagery.
When, in answer to Fay's letter of sexual invitation, Miss Lonelyhearts decides to telephone her, he pictures her as "a tent, hair-
covered and veined," and himself as a skeleton: "When he made
the skeleton enter the flesh tent, it flowered at every joint." Fay appears and is a giant: "legs like Indian clubs, breasts like balloons and
a brow like a pigeon." When he takes her arm, "It felt like a thigh."
Following her up the stairs to his apartment, "he watched the

action of her massive hams; they were like two enormous grindstones." Undressing, "she made sea sounds; something flapping like
a sail; there was the creak of ropes; then he heard the wave-against-
a-wharf smack of rubber on flesh. Her call for him to hurry was a
sea-moan, and when he lay beside her, she heaved, tidal, moon-
driven." Eventually Miss Lonelyhearts "crawled out of bed like
an exhausted swimmer leaving the surf," and she soon drags him
back.

If Fay is an oceanic monster, Peter Doyle is only a sinister puppy.
In bringing Miss Lonelyhearts back to the apartment at Fay's order,
he half-jokes, "Ain't I the pimp, to bring home a guy for my wife?"
Fay reacts by hitting him in the mouth with a rolled-up newspaper,
and his comic response is to growl like a dog and catch the paper
with his teeth. When she lets go of her end he drops to his hands
and knees and continues to imitate a dog on the floor. As Miss
Lonelyhearts leans over to help him up, "Doyle tore open Miss
Lonelyhearts fly, then rolled over on his back, laughing wildly."
Fay, more properly, accepts him as a dog and kicks him.

The obsessive theme of *Miss Lonelyhearts* is human pain and
suffering, but it is represented almost entirely as female suffering.
This is first spelled out in the letters addressed to Miss Lonelyhearts:
Sick-of-it-all is a Roman Catholic wife who has had seven children
in twelve years, is pregnant again, and has kidney pains so excru-
ciating that she cries all the time. Desperate is a sixteen-year-old
born with a hole in her face instead of a nose, who wants to have
dates like other girls. Harold S. writes about his thirteen-year-old
deaf-and-dumb sister Gracie, who was raped by a man when she
was playing on the roof, and who will be brutally punished if her
parents find out about it. Broad Shoulders was hit by a car when
she was first pregnant, and is alternately persecuted and deserted by
an unbalanced husband, in five pages of ghastly detail. Miss Lonelyhearts gets only two letters about male suffering, one from a paralyzed boy who wants to play the violin, the other from Peter Doyle,
who complains of the pain from his crippled leg and the general
meaninglessness of life.

The theme of indignities committed on women comes up in
another form in the stories Miss Lonelyheart's friends tell in

Delehanty's. They seem to be exclusively anecdotes of group rape, of one woman gang-raped by eight neighbors, of another kept in the back room of a speakeasy for three days, until "on the last day they sold tickets to niggers." Miss Lonelyhearts identifies himself with "wife-torturers, rapers of small children." At one point he tries giving his readers the traditional Christian justification for suffering, that it is Christ's gift to mankind to bring them to Him, but he tears up the column.

Ultimately the novel cannot justify or even explain suffering, only proclaim its omnipresence. Lying sick in bed, Miss Lonelyhearts gets a vision of human life: "He found himself in the window of a pawnshop full of fur coats, diamond rings, watches, shotguns, fishing tackle, mandolins. All these things were the paraphernalia of suffering. A tortured high light twisted on the blade of a gift knife, a battered horn grunted with pain." Finally his mind forms everything into a gigantic cross, and he falls asleep exhausted.

The book's desperate cry of pain and suffering comes to a focus in what Miss Lonelyhearts calls his "Christ complex." He recognizes that Christ is the only answer to his readers' letters, but that "if he did not want to get sick, he had to stay away from the Christ business. Besides, Christ was Shrike's particular joke." As Miss Lonelyhearts leaves the office and walks through a little park, the shadow of a lamppost pierces his side like a spear. Since nothing grows in the park's battered earth, he decides to ask his correspondents to come and water the soil with their tears. He imagines Shrike telling him to teach them to pray each morning, "Give us this day our daily stone," and thinks: "He had given his reader many stones; so many, in fact, that he had only one left—the stone that had formed in his gut."

Jesus Christ, Shrike says is "the Miss Lonelyhearts of Miss Lonelyhearts." Miss Lonelyhearts has nailed an ivory Christ to the wall of his room with great spikes, but it disappoints him: "Instead of writhing, the Christ remained calmly decorative." Miss Lonelyhearts recalls, "As a boy in his father's church, he had discovered that something stirred in him when he shouted the name of Christ, something secret and enormously powerful." Unfortunately, he recognizes, it is not faith but hysteria: "For him, Christ was the most natural of excitements."

Miss Lonelyhearts tells Betty he is "a humanity lover," but Shrike more aptly identifies him a "leper licker." "If he could only believe in Christ," Miss Lonelyhearts thinks "then everything would be simple and the letters extremely easy to answer." Later he recognizes that "Shrike had accelerated his sickness by teaching him to handle his one escape, Christ, with a thick glove of words." He decides that he has had a part in the general betrayal of suffering mankind: "The thing that made his share in it particularly bad was that he was capable of dreaming the Christ dream. He felt that he had failed at it, not so much because of Shrike's jokes or his own self-doubt, but because of his lack of humility." Miss Lonelyhearts concludes that "with him, even the word Christ was a vanity." When he gets drunk with Doyle, he calls on Christ joyously, and goes home with Doyle to bring the glad tidings to both Doyles, to heal their marriage. He preaches "love" to them and realizes that he is only writing another column, switches to preaching Christ Jesus, "the black fruit that hangs on the crosstree . . . the bidden fruit," and realizes that he is only echoing Shrike's poisoned rhetoric.

What Miss Lonelyhearts eventually achieves, since he cannot believe in the real Christ, and refuses to become a spurious Christ, is Peter's condition. He becomes the rock on which the new church will be founded, but it is the church of catatonic withdrawal. After three days in bed Miss Lonelyhearts attains a state of perfect calm, and the stone in his gut expands until he becomes "an ancient rock, smooth with experience." The Shrikes come to take him to a party at their apartment, and against this rock the waves of Shrike dash in vain. When Mary wriggles on Miss Lonelyhearts' lap in the cab, "the rock remained perfect." At the party he withstands Shrike's newest mockery, the Miss Lonelyhearts Game, with indifference: "What goes on in the sea is of no interest to the rock." Miss Lonelyhearts leaves the party with Betty: "She too should see the rock he had become." He shamelessly promises her marriage and domesticity: "The rock was a solidification of his feeling, his conscience, his sense of reality, his self-knowledge." He then goes back to his sickbed content: "The rock had been thoroughly tested and had been found perfect."

The next day Miss Lonelyhearts is burning with fever, and "the rock became a furnace." The room fills with grace, the illusory grace of madness, and as Doyle comes up the stairs with a pistol Miss Lonelyhearts rushes downstairs to embrace him and heal his crippled leg, a miracle that will embody his succoring all suffering mankind with love. Unable to escape Miss Lonelyhearts' mad embrace, terrified by Betty coming up the stairs, Doyle tries to toss away the gun, and Miss Lonelyhearts is accidentally shot. He falls dragging Doyle down the stairs in his arms.

It is of course a homosexual tableau—the men locked in embrace while the woman stands helplessly by—and behind his other miseries Miss Lonelyhearts has a powerful latent homosexuality. It is this that is ultimately the joke of his name and the book's title. It explains his acceptance of teasing dates with Mary and his coldness with Mary; he thinks of her excitement and notes: "No similar change ever took place in his own body, however. Like a dead man, only friction could make him warm or violence make him mobile." It explains his discontent with Betty. Most of all it explains his joy at being seduced by Fay—"He had always been the pursuer, but now found a strange pleasure in having the roles reversed"—and how quickly the pleasure turns to disgust.

The communion Miss Lonelyhearts achieves with Doyle in Delehanty's consists in their sitting silently holding hands, Miss Lonelyhearts pressing "with all the love he could manage" to overcome the revulsion he feels at Doyle's touch. Back at the Doyles, after Doyle has ripped open Miss Lonelyhearts' fly and been kicked by his wife, they hold hands again, and when Fay comes back in the room she says "What a sweet pair of fairies you guys are." It is West's ultimate irony that the symbolic embrace they manage at the end is one penetrating the body of the other with a bullet.

We could, if we so chose, write Miss Lonelyhearts' case history before the novel begins. Terrified of his stern religious father, identifying with his soft loving mother, the boy renounces his phallicism out of castration anxiety—a classic Oedipus complex. In these terms the Shrikes are Miss Lonelyhearts' Oedipal parents, abstracted as the father's loud voice and the mother's tantalizing breast. The scene at the end of Miss Lonelyhearts' date with Mary Shrike is horrifying and superb. Standing outside her apartment door, suddenly overcome with passion, he strips her naked under her fur coat while she keeps talking mindlessly of her mother's death, mumbling and repeating herself, so that Shrike will not hear their sudden silence and come out. Finally Mary agrees to let Miss Lonelyhearts in if Shrike is not home, goes inside, and soon Shrike peers out the door, wearing only the top of his pajamas. It is the child's Oedipal vision perfectly dramatized: he can clutch at his mother's body but loses her each time to his more potent rival.

It should be noted that if this is the pattern of Miss Lonelyhearts' Oedipus complex, it is not that of West, nor are the Shrikes the pattern of West's parents. How conscious was West of all or any of this? I would guess, from the book's title, that he was entirely conscious of at least Miss Lonelyhearts' latent homosexuality. As for the Oedipus complex, all one can do is note West's remarks in "Some Notes on Miss Lonelyhearts": "Psychology has nothing to do with reality nor should it be used as motivation. The novelist is no longer a psychologist. Psychology can become much more important. The great body of case histories can be used in the way the ancient writers use their myths. Freud is your Bulfinch; you can not learn from him."

The techniques West uses to express his themes are perfectly suited to them. The most important is a pervasive desperate and savage tone, not only in the imagery of violence and suffering, but everywhere. It is the tone of a world where unreason is triumphant. Telling Miss Lonelyhearts that he is awaiting a girl "of great intelligence," Shrike "illustrated the word *intelligence* by carving two enormous breasts in the air with his hands." When Miss Lonelyhearts is in the country with Betty, a gas station attendant tells him amiably that "it wasn't the hunters who drove out the deer, but the yids." When Miss Lonelyhearts accidentally collides with a man in Delehanty's and turns to apologize, he is punched in the mouth.

The flowering cactus that blooms in this wasteland is Shrike's rhetoric. The book begins with a mock prayer he has composed for

Miss Lonelyhearts, and every time Shrike appears he makes a masterly speech: on religion, on escapes, on the gospel of Miss Lonelyhearts according to Shrike. He composes a mock letter to God, in which Miss Lonelyhearts confesses shyly: "I read your column and like it very much." He is a cruel and relentless punster and wit. In his sadistic game at the party, Shrike reads aloud letters to Miss Lonelyhearts. He reads one from a pathetic old woman who sells pencils for a living, and concludes: "She has rheum in her eyes. Have you room in your heart for her?" He reads another, from the paralyzed boy who wants to play the violin, and concludes: "How pathetic! However, one can learn much from this parable. Label the boy Labor, the violin Capital, and so on . . ." Shrike's masterpiece, the brilliant evocation of the ultimate inadequacy of such escapes as the soil, the South Seas, Hedonism, and art, is a classic of modern rhetoric, as is his shorter speech on religion. Here are a few sentences from the latter: "Under the skin of man is a wondrous jungle where veins like lush tropical growths hang along overripe organs and weed-like entrails writhe in squirming tangles of red and yellow. In this jungle, flitting from rock-gray lungs to golden intestines, from liver to lights and back to liver again, lives a bird called the soul. The Catholic hunts this bird with bread and wine, the Hebrew with a golden ruler, the Protestant on leaden feet with leaden words, the Buddhist with gestures, the Negro with blood."

The other cactus that flowers in the wasteland is sadistic violence. The book's most harrowing chapter, "Miss Lonelyhearts and the Lamb," is a dream or recollection of a college escapade, in which Miss Lonelyhearts and two other boys, after drinking all night, buy a lamb to barbecue in the woods. Miss Lonelyhearts persuades his companions to sacrifice it to God before barbecuing it. They lay the lamb on a flower-covered altar and Miss Lonelyhearts tries to cut his throat, but succeeds only in maiming it and breaking the knife. The lamb escapes and crawls off into the underbrush, and the boys flee. Later Miss Lonelyhearts goes back and crushes the lamb's head with a stone. This nightmarish scene, with its unholy suggestions of the sacrifices of Isaac and Christ, embodies the book's bitter paradox: that sadism is the perversion of love.

Visiting Betty early in the novel, aware "that only violence could make him supple," Miss Lonelyhearts reaches inside her robe and tugs at her nipple unpleasantly. "Let me pluck this rose," he says, "I want to wear it in my buttonhole." In "Miss Lonelyhearts and the Clean Old Man," he and a drunken friend find an old gentleman in a washroom, drag him to a speakeasy, and torment him with questions about his "homosexualistic tendencies." As they get nastier and nastier, Miss Lonelyhearts feels "as he had felt years before, when he had accidentally stepped on a small frog. Its spilled guts had filled him with pity, but when its suffering had become real to his senses, his pity had turned to rage and he had beaten it frantically until it was dead." He ends by twisting the old man's arm until the old man screams and someone hits Miss Lonelyhearts with a chair.

The book's only interval of decency, beauty, and peace is the pastoral idyll of the few days Miss Lonelyhearts spends with Betty in the country. They drive in a borrowed car to the deserted farmhouse in Connecticut where she was born. It is spring, and Miss Lonelyhearts "had to admit, even to himself, that the pale new leaves, shaped and colored like candle flames, were beautiful and that the air smelt clean and alive." They work at cleaning up the place, Betty cooks simple meals, and they go down to the pond to watch the deer. After they eat an apple that has ominous Biblical overtones, Betty reveals that she is a virgin and they go fraternally to bed. The next day they go for a naked swim; then, with "no wind to disturb the pull of the earth," Betty is ceremonially deflowered on the new grass. The reader is repeatedly warned that natural innocence cannot save Miss Lonelyhearts: the noise of birds and crickets is "a horrible racket" in his ears; in the woods, "in the deep shade there was nothing but death—rotten leaves, gray and white fungi, and over everything a funereal hush." When they get back to New York, "Miss Lonelyhearts knew that Betty had failed to cure him and that he had been right when he had said that he could never forget the letters." Later when Miss Lonelyhearts is a rock and leaves Shrike's party with Betty, he tries to create a miniature idyll of innocence by taking her out for a strawberry soda, but it fails. Pregnant by him and intending to have an abortion,

Betty remains nevertheless in Edenic innocence; Miss Lonelyhearts is irretrievably fallen, and there is no savior who can redeem.

The book's pace is frantic and its imagery is garish, ugly, and compelling. The letters to Miss Lonelyhearts are "stamped from the dough of suffering with a heart-shaped cookie knife." The sky looks "as if it had been rubbed with a soiled eraser." A bloodshot eye in the peephole of Delehanty's glows "like a ruby in an antique iron ring." Finishing his sermon to the "intelligent" girl, Shrike "buried his triangular face like the blade of a hatchet in her neck." Miss Lonelyhearts' tongue is "a fat thumb," his heart "a congealed lump of icy fat," and his only feeling "icy fatness." Goldsmith, a colleague at the paper, has cheeks "like twin rolls of smooth pink toilet paper." Only the imagery of the Connecticut interlude temporarily thaws the iciness and erases the unpleasant associations with fatness and thumb. As Miss Lonelyhearts watches Betty naked, "She looked a little fat, but when she lifted something to the line, all the fat disappeared. Her raised arms pulled her breasts up until they were like pink-tipped thumbs."

The unique greatness of *Miss Lonelyhearts* seems to have come into the world with hardly a predecessor, but it has itself influenced a great many American novelists since. *Miss Lonelyhearts* seems to me one of the three finest American novels of our century. The other two are F. Scott Fitzgerald's *The Great Gatsby* and Ernest Hemingway's *The Sun Also Rises*. It shares with them a lost and victimized hero, a bitter sense of our civilization's falsity, a pervasive melancholy atmosphere of failure and defeat. If the tone of *Miss Lonelyhearts* is more strident, its images more garish, its pace more rapid and hysterical, it is as fitting as epitome of the thirties as they are of the twenties. If nothing in the forties and fifties has similarly gone beyond *Miss Lonelyhearts* in violence and shock, it may be because it stands at the end of the line.

The Waste Land of Nathanael West

by Edmond L. Volpe

Nathanael West's *Miss Lonelyhearts* has too long been denied recognition as one of the great short novels in American Literature. West's masterful use of poetic imagery in the novel form is incisive, brilliant; his story is powerful, its emotional impact overwhelming, its significance profound. Technically, the novel is marred, to some extent, by a loss of artistic control in the final chapters, but despite this flaw, the book deserves a niche in the history of American Literature, not only on the basis of literary merit, but also because it is the answer of the 1930's to the great poem of the 1920's—T. S. Eliot's *The Waste Land*. I do not know whether West intended his novel as a reply to Eliot. The similarities in theme and imagery seem too obvious to be accidental. West's intentions, at any rate, are of little significance: his novel is an answer to the optimism implicit in Eliot's vision of man and society. Though Eliot's poem is a somber and depressing view of modern man and his culture, it is a view brightened by hope. Eliot's optimism is particularly obvious when his vision is contrasted with West's.

The unnamed protagonist of *The Waste Land* (West's protagonist, too, is unnamed, though in an earlier version published in part in *Contact,* he is named) is throughout the novel on a pilgrimage. He moves through the waste land of his soul and of his society seeking salvation. The land he inhabits is a world without values, a mechanical world reflecting the aridity in the soul of modern man. There were times in human history, the poem informs us, when

"*The Waste Land of Nathanael West*" by Edmond L. Volpe. From Rena-scence, *13* (*1961*); *69–77, and 112. Reprinted by permission of the author and the editors.*

man was vibrant with life: he had ideals, moral values and re-
sponded to basic natural forces. Modern man, however, is sexually
impotent, morally sterile, culturally stagnant. He is a mechanical
man, physically alive, spiritually dead. The land is arid because
man's soul is arid. Since the Waste Land is man-made, it is within
man's power to regenerate his dead world. In the final section of
the poem, the protagonist discovers the means of salvation—religious belief. Though he is not yet ready to achieve his salvation,
the method is available to him. Eliot's Waste Land is not the
product of forces beyond human control. There is supreme order
in the universe. Man, individually, need only submit to God, the
source of that order. By submitting, man can bring order into his
own soul and thereby into his world.

As depressing as Eliot's vision may be, therefore, it is far from
pessimistic. West's vision, in contrast, is terrifyingly pessimitic. His
waste land, which is symbolized in part by the park between the
newspaper office and the speakeasy, in many ways resembles Eliot's:
"As far as he could discover, there were no signs of spring. The decay that covered the surface of the mottled ground was not the
kind in which life generates. Last year, he remembered, May had
failed to quicken these soiled fields. It had taken all the brutality
of July to torture a few green spikes through the exhausted dirt."

It, too, is a spiritually barren world in which an adding machine
ritual replaces older religions, a culturally sterile land in which
the people "have dissipated their radical energy in an orgy of
stone breaking." The inhabitants of West's waste land, as I shall
presently show, are similar to the inhabitants of Eliot's. The major
differences in the two visions is in the cause of the cultural and
moral aridity. To West, the human being appears a misfit in an
undirected universe: "Man has a tropism for order. . . . The
physical world has a tropism for disorder, entrophy." Man cannot
impose order on the universe. With his dreams—his religions, his
philosophies, his art, his science—he has tried to establish order,
but history and time have proved his efforts futile. Evil, the manifestation of the world's disorder in human existence, has always
flourished. The heroic ages Eliot recalls in his poem are for West
simply periods in which men's illusions and dreams were more

powerful, and therefore more effective in disguising the realities. And the realities in human existence are the entropy of the physical world and man's supreme need for order. But every "order has within it the germ of destruction. All order is doomed, yet the battle is worth while."

The battle is the alternative to suicide, but how does man battle? "Men have always fought their misery with dreams." West's tragic vision of human life is the same vision Eugene O'Neil dramatized in *The Iceman Cometh,* probably the most despairing play of our time. Both writers see man's ideals and ideas as nothing but pipe dreams. These empty dreams, as man's only defense against the brutality of reality, are essential if he is to go on living.

I make much of West's despair because it is the fact that eluded me when I first read *Miss Lonelyhearts.* The columnist's plight is so pathetic, his desire to succor his fellow sufferers so attractive, his Christ dream so appealing that he remains a sympathetic character to the end of the novel. Miss Lonelyhearts in the final chapters, however, is a madman; he has severed all contact with reality. The theme of the novel demands that the reader experience pity, not sympathy, for Miss Lonelyhearts in his madness; but West, in his final chapters, does not exert sufficient artistic control over his story and his own feelings (I suspect) to withdraw his reader to an observer's position. Let me document these general statements by analyzing the novel.

Like Eliot's protagonist, the hero of *Miss Lonelyhearts* is given the opportunity to view the waste land in which he lives. What both protagonists see, as I indicated previously, is a world without values. There is one major difference: Miss Lonelyhearts' world has no values, not because man has thrown them over, substituting superficial values for good ones, but because the human being has reached a time in his history when he can no longer delude himself. None of his philosophies or dreams has ameliorated or accounted for the presence of evil, for the pain, the suffering, the misery of human existence. In the three letters that open the novel, the writers are victims, completely innocent victims, of forces beyond their control. They in no way deserve the suffering they are undergoing. Sick-of-it-all is being tortured by her husband, whose blind faith in

Catholicism has made him the destructive agent of a concept. Religion, which should be providing Sick-of-it-all comfort in her distress and a reason for living, is destroying her. Desperate is born without a nose. She pleads with Miss Lonelyhearts to tell her why she deserves such a fate. Harold S. begs advice about his deaf and dumb thirteen year old sister who has been raped by a stranger and is now to suffer the social humiliation of an unwed mother. Each letter describes a natural or human force of evil that crushes man in a vise of anguish. For these sufferers the flame of their agony is reality. Their protective illusions have burned away. But reality cannot be endured without dreams, and in desperation the anguished victims write to Miss Lonelyhearts. The unknown writer of the newspaper column becomes their only hope of salvation; in his column they seek "The Word."

Miss Lonelyhearts' waste land, therefore, is more than a reflection of man's personal and cultural degeneration; it is a land in which evil and human suffering stalk in their naked horror. No sensitive viewer of this land can observe the anguish and retain his sanity. The inhabitants of the waste land are, from necessity, breathing dead men. The death mask is their alternative to facing the horrors of life. The chief spokesman of these inhabitants is Shrike, named for the butcher bird that impales its prey on a thorn or twig while tearing it apart with its sharp hooked beak. Shrike is a "dead pan . . . his features huddled together in a dead, gray triangle," one of the crowd flowing over London bridge in Eliot's "Unreal City" passage. Shrike, like all human beings, must have some defense against reality. One of the nasty products of "this unbelieving age," he lives by impaling the dreams of others and ripping them apart: he makes a joke of everything. He and his fellow newspapermen had "believed in literature, had believed in Beauty and in personal expression as an absolute end. When they lost this belief, they lost everything." Their dream destroyed, they became "machines for making jokes. . . . They, no matter what the motivating force, death, love, or God, made jokes." Shrike's wife, Mary (Belladonna, the Lady of the Rocks), is incapable of giving herself sexually, and her husband, in love with her, comforts himself with cruel jokes and with the sterile sex of the "Miss Farkises of this world" who "had long legs, thick ankles, big hands, a powerful body, a slender neck and a childish face made tiny by a man's haircut."

Miss Lonelyhearts, too, had been a joke machine until the column he had begun as a joke forced him "to examine the values by which he lives. This examination shows him that he is the victim of the joke and not its perpetrator." He is the victim because the people he had planned to laugh at reveal to him the horrors of life; their agonized pleas penetrate to his heart. He can no longer ignore the reality of human existence. Like Melville's Captain Ahab, West's Miss Lonelyhearts concludes that there is no such thing as justice in the universe; human evil is merely an eruption of universal evil. The two characters experience the same awful insight. Their subsequent madness takes different forms because they are a century apart in the history of man. There is no fight in the twentieth century columnist, no need for vegeance. Captain Ahab had something to hate, something to struggle against. He could defy the gods, hate the injustice of the universe, reject the cruelty of man. Miss Lonelyhearts has no opponent: "He searched the sky for a target. But the gray sky looked as if it had been rubbed with a soiled eraser. It held no angels, flaming crosses, olive-bearing doves, wheels within wheels. Only a newspaper struggled in the air like a kite with a broken spine."

There is nothing to blame, no God to hold responsible. By becoming Miss Lonelyhearts, the newspaperman had drawn back his protective curtain of illusion. The sight of naked horror the letters bring to his view destroys his mental and emotional stability, placing him on the very edge of madness. When he looks up to the sky for a target and can find none, Miss Lonelyhearts has reached that moment of complete despair that the French existentialist writers a few years later were to term *Nauseé,* or The Absurd. Miss Lonelyhearts' creator, however, was no existenialist. He could not move out of his despair; he could only joke about man's attempt to curtain reality, write a satire on the Christ dream—the salvation of Eliot's Waste Land.

On the edge of madness when the novel opens, Miss Lonelyhearts struggles to save himself. Two methods of salvation are available to him. He can try to ignore the sight he has seen and forget it in some personal escape dream; or he can face the horror and try to bring solace to the sufferers by providing them with some dream to replace those they have lost. His sensitivity and sympathetic nature force him to take this latter method. He realizes that he shall never be able to forget the pain he has witnessed. The columnist is a reader of the *Brothers Karamazov;* Father Zossima's advice, to love man even in his sin, excites him. He envisions himself teaching the whole world to love. Man would no longer be cruel. "The kingdom of Heaven would arrive. He would sit on the right hand of the Lamb." Also, Miss Lonelyhearts is the son of a minister. "As a boy in his father's church, he had discovered that something stirred in him when he shouted the name of Christ, something secret and enormously powerful. He had played with this thing, but had never allowed it to come alive." Miss Lonelyhearts, therefore, has a readily available emotional recourse in his moment of need. "He knew now what this thing was—hysteria, a snake whose scales are tiny mirrors in which the dead world takes on a semblance of life. And how dead the world is . . . a world of doorknobs. He wondered if hysteria were really too steep a price to pay for bringing it to life."

The Christ dream for Miss Lonelyhearts, in other words, is a form of madness; it can cut him off from reality, making the dead world seem alive. As a product of his age, however, Miss Lonelyhearts cannot rationally accept Christ, and religion is meaningless to him. In a dream sequence, his desire to help his fellow men and his inability to accept religon as a means of salvation are symbolized. He first sees himself as a magician on a stage, performing tricks with doorknobs (dreams). He is successful with his tricks, but when he tries to lead his audience in prayer the only prayer that comes to mind is a cynical parody that Shrike, who echoed Miss Lonelyhearts' rational self, had taught him. In his first dream the columnist desires to lead his audience out of the waste land, but he cannot because he lacks conviction. In the second dream scene the ritual of animal sacrifice (reminiscent of the primitive rites referred to by Eliot) is no recourse for modern man. Miss Lonelyhearts and the two college companions with whom he had been arguing about the existence of God are unable to perform the sacrificial ceremony.

Out of pity Miss Lonelyhearts goes back to kill with a stone (throughout the novel a symbol of despair) the wounded lamb, the traditional symbol of Christ.

Miss Lonelyhearts knows, therefore, that if he gives himself over to the Christ dream he will be cutting himself off from reality. But what else can he offer Sick-of-it-all and Broken Hearted, whose own dreams have evaporated in the hellish flames of reality? He is their last hope, and he cannot ignore them. He must help his fellow men, suffer for them, become the living Christ. Christ is his natural inevitable haven, though he realizes it is an empty dream. Christ, as Shrike declares, is the Miss Lonelyhearts of Miss Lonelyhearts—the ultimate, vacuous hope of the desperate. The columnist also knows that "Even if he were to have a genuine religious experience, it would be personal and so meaningless, except to a psychologist." The Christ dream, Nathanael West is saying, can perhaps provide personal escape, but it is not the salvation of the waste land; it is not, as in Eliot's poetry, the means of personal and thereby universal salvation.

The intensity of Miss Lonelyhearts' need drives him toward the Christ dream; the knowledge that Christ is no more than a dream drives him away. Torn in two, he moves toward the abyss of madness. He hesitates before he plunges over the brink, wondering if hysteria—madness—is too steep a price to pay. Eventually he realizes it is not, but first he tries a series of personal escapes, all of which fail because he cannot forget the cries of anguish and choke off his need to help his fellow men.

He goes to visit Betty, his fiancée. The visit is a failure; Betty and her ordered life are intolerable to him because her "sureness was based on the power to limit experience arbitrarily. Moreover, his confusion was significant, while her order was not." Betty, whom Chance has spared, lives within a tiny bright circle of personal peace by ignoring the shadows that surround her. She refuses to acknowledge the existence of evil. " 'No morality, only medicine,' " says Miss Lonelyhearts, describing her attitude. Human cruelty is not a manifestation of evil for Betty; it is sickness. And sickness can be cured. There is nothing fundamentally wrong with the universe; there are only minor aberrations.

Betty provides no escape, so at Delehanty's the columnist tries alcohol. Temporarily it is successful; he slips into a genial haze that makes him immune to the jokes of his fellow drinkers. He remembers an incident from his childhood: he is playing the piano and his sister responding happily to the music. He envisions children everywhere dancing in ordered natural motions of happiness. The thought of children revives the Christ dream. Reality shatters the moment of peace. He is punched in the mouth by a man whom he accidentally bumps as he turns from the bar. Miss Lonelyhearts becomes angry with himself for giving in to the dream. And at the end of the dunken evening he meets an aged homosexual. Alcohol has not blunted his sensitivity to suffering and he reacts as he had done many years before when he accidentally stepped on a small frog. "Its spilled guts had filled him with pity, but when its suffering had become real to his senses, his pity had turned to rage and he had beaten it frantically until it was dead." And so he beats up the pervert, trying symbolically to erase the suffering he can do nothing to lessen.

Alcohol fails to relieve his agony and so does his next attempt at escape—sex. For Mary Shrike, sex can be nothing but an unending game. Though Miss Lonelyhearts has played the sterile game with her before, in desperation—but without desire—he plays the game once more. To some extent he succeeds in shutting out the rest of the world. "He feels an icy fatness around his heart." The thought that the nightclub they go to is simply a more expensive type of dream than those offered by advertisements to develop biceps or busts merely irritates him. "For the time being, dreams left him cold." But he cannot escape. His sexual advances are countered with dreams. Mary talks of her parents, of her mother's death, of her father. "Parents are also part of the business of dreams. . . . People like Mary were unable to do without such tales." For a moment before Miss Lonelyhearts leaves Mary, he almost loses himself in awakened desire. The game ends; Mary rushes into her apartment where Shrike awaits her.

The next day at his desk, Miss Lonelyhearts envisions a desert of rust and body dirt in which Desperate and Broken Hearted are forming the letters of Miss Lonelyhearts' name with white-washed clam shells, products of the sea, the symbol of rebirth, regeneration. He reads Fay Doyle's letter, tries to "discover a moral reason" for not responding to her invitation, concluding that if "he could only believe in Christ, then adultery would be a sin, then everything would be simple and the letters extremely easy to answer." He cannot. He dismisses his Christ dream and tries sex once again. The meeting with Mrs. Doyle is reminiscent of the fertility rites Eliot makes allusions to in his poem, in which water serves as the regenerating medium. Mrs. Doyle is the sea, Miss Lonelyhearts the carcass thrown into the water. "She made sea sounds. . . . Her call to him to hurry was a sea-moan, and when he lay beside her, she heaved, tidal, moon-driven. Some fifteen minutes later, he crawled out of bed like an exhausted swimmer leaving the surf."

The ritual fails; sex is no escape for him or for Mrs. Doyle. Sitting on his lap, she tells him her life story and the "life out of which she spoke was even heavier than her body. It was as if a gigantic, living Miss Lonelyhearts letter in the shape of a paper weight had been placed in his brain."

This failure pushes Miss Lonelyhearts closer to madness. He becomes physically ill and spends two days in bed. He recognizes, however, that his "present sickness was unimportant. It was merely a trick of his body to relieve one more profound." His tension has increased. He pictures himself before the show window of a pawn shop, and with the forsaken possessions of the desperate he builds a phallus, a heart, a diamond, a circle, triangle, square, swastika, the symbols of men's dreams that have failed. "But nothing proved definitive, and he began to make a gigantic cross." He moves the cross to the ocean and adds to it with the refuse of the sea.

Betty comes to offer him an escape to simple country life, away from the city where so much human misery is concentrated. Another visitor, Shrike, arrives to describe with cynical eloquence and dismiss with cynical eloquence all the personal means of salvation available to Miss Lonelyhearts: the simple country life and absorption in the basic rhythm of nature, the South Sea Islands, the pursuit of pleasure, art, suicide, and drugs. None of these escapes can serve the sick man. As he listens, he thinks of "how Shrike had accelerated his sickness by teaching him to handle his one escape, Christ, with a thick glove of words."

Miss Lonelyhearts is ready now to give in to the hysteria. Betty, however, insists that he try the country life. He accompanies her to the Connecticut farm and for a few days he does know a measure of tranquility, even sexual satisfaction. He has entered, momentarily, Betty's world of limited experience. As soon, however, as they reach the Bronx slums on their return drive, "Miss Lonelyhearts knew that Betty had failed to cure him and that he had been right when he had said that he could never forget the letters."

Salvation that does nothing to ameliorate the general suffering is not for him. The Christ dream with its promise of universal love and universal salvation must be his dream. To placate his rational self, Miss Lonelyhearts, prodded "by his conscience . . . began to generalize. . . . Although dreams were once powerful, they have been made puerile by the movies, radio, and newspapers. Among many betrayals, this one is the worst. The thing that made his share in it particularly bad was that he was capable of dreaming the Christ dream. He felt he had failed at it, not so much because of Shrike's jokes or his own self-doubt, but because of his lack of humility."

The sick man is close to his release from reality. Humility and brotherly love flood his heart. Momentarily successful in his endeavor to surround everyone with love when Fay Doyle's crippled husband appeals to him for help in Delehanty's, Miss Lonelyhearts attempts to extend his success and unite the husband and wife with love. His failure is comically tragic. During the supper, he envelops them with his beatific smile, ignoing Fay's hand on his thigh beneath the table. He searches for a message that will convey his dream, that will bring the Kingdom of Heaven to the estranged couple. His words embarrass the Doyles. "By avoiding God, he had failed to tap the force in his heart and had merely written a column for his paper." A second more hysterical message makes him feel like "an empty bottle, shiny and sterile." His own salvation, the Christ dream, cannot be communicated. His dream is menaced by Fay who thrusts herself at him and makes him feel like "an empty bottle that is being slowly filled with warm, dirty water." Miss Lonelyhearts staves off this intrusion of reality by beating Fay Doyle until she releases her hold on him.

The columnist's growing spiritual isolation is reflected in his physical separation from the world. He jams his telephone and locks himself in his cell-like room. His only nourishment is crackers and water. ("When they ask for bread don't give them crackers as does the Church," Shrike had joked.) At the end of the three days of symbolic entombment, Miss Lonelyhearts arises. His suffering is over; he has become the rock. West's use here of the symbol of despair, the rock, to symbolize his protagonist's withdrawal from reality makes clear his attitude toward the Christ dream. (The symbol may also be a satirical reference to the effectiveness of the Church in aiding suffering mankind.) And the sea, the regenerative symbol, is now, ironically, applied to the world from which Miss Lonelyhearts has withdrawn.

The rock is twice tested. Shrike dashes into the sick man's room, "but fell back, as a wave that dashes against an ancient rock, smooth with experience, falls back." Shrike's jokes, which had become increasingly cynical as Miss Lonelyhearts moved deeper into his dream, reached their climax with the Miss Lonelyhearts game, a cruel, inhuman, gigantic joke with the columnist as its butt. Miss Lonelyhearts is impregnable. "What goes on in the sea is of no interest to the rock." The second trial is more severe. Betty is pregnant and announces she wants an abortion. Her fiancé argues against it, asks her to marry him, promises to give up his column, leave the newspaper, and accept her world of limited experience. He tells her everything she wants to hear, lying blithely, feeling no remorse. "He did not feel guilty. He did not feel. The rock was a solidification of his feeling, his conscience, his sense of reality, his self-knowledge." Though Miss Lonelyhearts' withdrawal from life is complete, his absorption in the Christ dream has one final phase. The next day the columnist becomes feverish; he hears the voice of God and, submitting, he achieves the peace which passeth understanding. (Eliot: "Then spoke the thunder . . . *Datta*") His "identification with God was complete. His heart was the one heart, the heart of God." West's next sentence, as a prelude to Miss Lonelyhearts' final act, is brutally ironic: "And his brain was likewise God's."

When Miss Lonelyhearts hears Peter Doyle toiling up the stairs, he rushes from his room with outspread arms to perform a miracle. He will make the crippled man whole as he, a spiritual cripple, has been made whole. The Christ dream has become a delusion: Miss Lonelyhearts is mad. Mistaking Doyle's cry of warning as an anguished plea for help, he runs to succor the cripple and all the other sufferers of the world. Frightened, Doyle turns to escape. Miss Lonelyhearts grabs him. When Betty enters, Doyle tries to get rid of the pistol wrapped in newspaper. The gun goes off; the columnist falls. The shooting lacks the dignity of a deliberate act; it is accidental: order cannot be imposed on a world that has a tropism for disorder.

Nathanael West keeps his point of view intact throughout his novel except in one scene: that in which Miss Lonelyhearts slips away from Shrike's party. The single, sudden shift away from the consciousness of Miss Lonelyhearts may have been designed to withdraw the reader's sympathy from the protagonist. The artistic maneuver fails; the inhumanity of Shrike's joke is far more repulsive than Miss Lonelyhearts' delusion. When the reader is returned in the next scene to the hero's consciousness, he is more inclined to sympathy than before, a feeling, I imagine, that West himself had and could not control. The artistry of most of the novel is so deliberate that one is forced to conclude that these final chapters are confused because West was strongly attracted to, even if he could not believe in it, the Christ dream. Despite the confusion, West does make clear his intentions and his theme.

Miss Lonelyhearts is a brilliant, profound expression of despair, able, a quarter century later, to evoke the feeling and mood of its period better than any other novel, including *The Sun Also Rises*. Reading the novel is a painful emotional experience, not unlike that produced by reading *The Waste Land*. But in Eliot's Waste Land regeneration is possible; in West's there is no hope of salvation.

PART TWO

View Points

Randall Reid: No Redeemer, No Promised Land

The world of Miss Lonelyhearts is a waste land.[1] Its psychology owes far more to regenerative myths than to Freud and far more to ascetic or apocalyptic Christianity than to Jessie L. Weston. The world confirms the saint's anguished vision of this life. It reaches but to dust. Nature and sexuality are agents of death, alive only in their power to hurt. Though latent homosexuality is not relevant to the novel's major themes, universally crippled and malignant sexuality is. The two representatives of fleshly love—Shrike and Mrs. Doyle—are described in imagery which is grotesquely symbolic. Shrike's name, for example, comes from the butcher bird which impales its living prey on thorns, and the sense of murderous penetration is in his every act. Mrs. Doyle, however, is omnivorously engulfing. The sexes are thereby given nightmarish attributes: the phallus is just an instrument of sadistic impalment, and the female genitalia are a smothering, swallowing, devouring sea. Miss Lonelyhearts is quite properly terrified of both sexes. And quite properly sympathetic to both. Like all the other forces in the novel, the sexes are, in their active forms, irreconcilable and mutually destructive. But in their passive forms, both sexes are victims—Doyle, Mary Shrike, the idiot girl, even Shrike himself. " 'She's selfish. She's a damned selfish bitch. . . . Sleeping with her is like sleeping with a knife in one's groin.' " (P. 84.) Miss Lonelyhearts is there-

---

"No Redeemer, No Promised Land." From The Fiction of Nathanael West: No Redeemer, No Promised Land *by Reid Randall (Chicago and London: University of Chicago Press, 1967), pp. 82–83, 85–87. Copyright © 1967 by University of Chicago Press. Reprinted by permission of the publisher.*

[1] The basic waste-land image obviously derives from Eliot. Edmond L. Volpe has even argued that *Miss Lonelyhearts* is consciously "an answer to the optimism implicit in Eliot's vision of man and society." See Volpe, "The Waste Land of Nathanael West."

fore like a child with parents so vicious and so unhappy that identifying with either sex is impossible. And, conversely, identifying
with both is inevitable. He is the child in whom all the destructive
and conflicting demands of the parents meet. Unless he can reconcile the sexes to each other, they will destroy themselves and him.
His own sexual behavior exhibits the same duality of active cruelty and passive suffering. With both Mary Shrike and Betty, for
example, he is sometimes as compulsively destructive as Shrike.
Sexuality therefore arouses in Miss Lonelyhearts both personal
terror and moral horror. His acceptance of "castration" at the moment of conversion is a fantasy of deliverance, not a resignation
to loss.

There is, in the saint's vision, no real love but divine love, no
real life but eternal life. When God is withdrawn, only deadness
remains. . . .

The Comic Strip Novel

I can't do a review of *Miss Lonelyhearts,* but here, at random, are
some of the things I thought when writing it:

As subtitle: "A novel in the form of a comic strip." The chapters
to be squares in which many things happen through one action.
The speeches contained in the conventional balloons. I abandoned
this idea, but retained some of the comic strip technique: Each
chapter instead of going forward in time, also goes backward, forward,
up and down in space like a picture. Violent images are used to
illustrate commonplace events. Violent acts are left almost bald.—
West, "Some Notes on Miss Lonelyhearts." [2]

A novel in the form of a comic strip was not as strange a notion
as it may seem. West was always fascinated by painting and caricature,[3] and of course popular art was, in intellectual circles of
the twenties, as fashionable as the fox-trot. Carl Van Vechten was
exploring Harlem, E. E. Cummings was firing off salutes to bur-

---

[2] West, "Some Notes on Miss Lonelyhearts," p. 1.

[3] It may even be worth remembering that S. J. Perelman, West's friend and
brother-in-law, began as a cartoonist and that West himself drew the first cover
design for his college literary magazine.

lesque, and Gilbert Seldes was proclaiming that Charlie Chaplin and George Herriman (the creator of Krazy Kat) were the two greatest artists in America.[4] The distinctive forms which emerged —movies and comic strips—were both picture narratives. And the union of word and picture was not limited to popular art. The surrealists often used pictorial representations of literary ideas, and even Rimbaud, according to Verlaine, had formed and titled his *Illuminations* after the cheap colored prints which delighted him.[5]

Another fashionable experiment in picture narrative is now almost forgotten—the wordless "novels" in woodcuts of Lynd Ward. *God's Man* and *Madman's Drum* both preceded *Miss Lonelyhearts* by three years. Ward was not of course a particularly impressive pioneer. His style was commercial, and *God's Man*[6] is just a banal and melodramatic parable of the artist's fate. *Madman's Drum*,[7] however, is fairly interesting in itself and curiously similar to *Miss Lonelyhearts*. West's description of Miss Lonelyhearts exactly matches the puritan hero's countenance in *Madman's Drum:* "No one could fail to recognize the New England puritan. His forehead was high and narrow. His nose was long and fleshless. His bony chin was shaped and cleft like a hoof." (P. 18). In one of Ward's woodcuts, the hero is profiled against a shadowed wall where a crucifix hangs, looking very much like Miss Lonelyhearts in his room. In another, a seducer buries his sharp chin in the neck of his victim. Even the plot of *Madman's Drum* bears a general resemblance to the plot of *Miss Lonelyhearts*. Abandoning the religion of his ancestors, the hero successively seeks meaning or happi-

[4] Gilbert Seldes, *The Seven Lively Arts* [New York: Harper and Brothers, 1924], p. 50.

[5] Louise Varèse, Introduction to [Rimbaud's] *Illuminations and Other Prose Poems*, trans. Louise Varèse [New York: New Directions Paperbacks, 1967], pp. x–xii.

[6] Lynd Ward, *God's Man: A Novel in Woodcuts*.

[7] Lynd Ward, *Madman's Drum: A Novel in Woodcuts*. I have no proof that West knew Ward's books at the time he was writing *Miss Lonelyhearts*, though West's interest in the graphic arts and Ward's prominence at the time make it likely that he did. Ward was a frequent contributor to several periodicals, including *Americana*, whose staff West joined a few months after the publication of *Miss Lonelyhearts*. See Light, p. 103.

ness in philosophy, astronomy, marriage, fatherhood, social action. He fails disastrously in each attempt and ends by embracing madness.

Ward entirely lacked West's subtlety and comic sense, but his techniques, even when crude, suggest more possibilities than Ward himself explored. He necessarily used the devices which any wordless story must: a plot reduced to allegorical simplicity, stereotyped characters whose features are exaggerated into masks, and physical actions which become, in the absence of words, violent expressive gestures. He used, that is, the conventions which visual media always use. Grotesque masks and violent action are in the standard repertoire of slapstick and pantomime—of Punch and Judy, circus clowns, Keystone cops. When there are no words, gesture and expression must carry everything; violence becomes a form of ballet. In the semiwordless medium of the comic strip, however, gesture is discontinuous. Both words and actions are fragmentary and overburdened. Dialogue must be compressed into a single speech which in turn must be squeezed into a balloon; action must be revealed in a snapshot image. Under the double pressure of insufficient words and static pictures, violence again becomes a necessary convention, but now the choreographic action of pantomime must yield to images which are as formal and condensed as hieroglyphs. Cartoon panels typically end with exactly that kind of image— with Snuffy Smith sailing over a fence bearing the print of a mule's hoofs on his rump or with Ignatz bouncing a brick off Krazy Kat. In *Miss Lonelyhearts,* West also used violent images as hieroglyphs. When Shrike buries "his triangular face like the blade of a hatchet in [Miss Farkis'] neck" (p. 33), the image reveals the climax of a particular episode, the sadism inherent in all Shrike's actions, and the destructiveness which pervades sexuality throughout the novel. And of course nearly every episode does end in a revelatory and violent image—the sacrifice of the lamb, the torture of the clean old man, the sexual union of Miss Lonelyhearts and Betty in the country. As West said, "Violent images are used to illustrate commonplace events. Violent acts are left almost bald."

Josephine Herbst: *Miss Lonelyhearts*: An Allegory

Miss Lonelyhearts reads like a detective story. Its realism is not concerned with actuality but with the comprehension of a reality beyond reality. The furniture of the speakeasy, the upside-down quality of New York night and day life provide a background that only a fine movie camera could actually interpret. This crazy pattern fits the nightmare quality of the story of Miss Lonelyhearts, the newspaper columnist, who under a sentimental name acts high priest to the broken hearted whose letters begging advice pour into his sanctum. Actually *Miss Lonelyhearts,* the book, is a sort of allegory.

Miss Lonelyhearts floundering among the problems of humanity, stuck in the Slough of Despond of bankrupt emotionalism to the accompaniment of high powered motors, jazz music, weeping drunks and men out-of-work reflects much more than his own minute destiny. The entire jumble of modern society, bankrupt not only in cash but more tragically in emotion, is depicted here like a life sized engraving narrowed down to the head of a pin. Miss Lonelyhearts stricken with the suffering of the underdog, seeks an answer. Flagellating himself with suffering, he in turn incurs suffering. His sadism breeds back upon himself and in bewilderment he turns to God, symbol of crucifixion and death. The pathological intensity of this seeking leads him to the desire to embrace humanity and that embrace pitches him to death. The ecstatic moment, realistically furnished, in which this occurs approaches the miracle of the old Mystery Plays.

It is significant that although all the scenes are not night scenes, in retrospect they appear to take place in semi-darkness, in that sort of twilight that occurs in dreams. The characters too are those of the dream, faces out of line, some distortion. Miss Lonelyhearts himself, in his dilemma, seeking a way out, is without distinct

"*Miss Lonelyhearts: An Allegory*" by *Josephine Herbst. From* **Contempo** *3 (July 25, 1933), 11. Reprinted by permission of the author.*

features. As he goes down, he seems to be someone wearing the huge nose of a clown who has been tightropewalking and has suddenly been discovered to have broken legs. He falls into the pit and even as he sinks the clown nose tortures us with a desire to laugh, the same kind of laughter that hysterically crops up in a tragic moment. If the characters are not sharpened in an individualistic way it is because they much more nearly serve their purpose in this book as types. They are not Mrs. Jones or Miss Smith or Mr. Brown but the Desolates, the Heartaches, the Anxious of the world whose faces mask identical suffering more poignant than any individual difference.

Doomed by the society that roars around them to live ignominiously and alone in rabbit hutches, poking their heads out to wail to their father confessor, who, like them is lost, they are not puppets so much as they are representatives of a great Distress. Let anyone who thinks this implies a grotesqueness out of line with the strictest contemporary reality pick up any newspaper. Terror accompanied by the great wash of indifference is in every line. The Tom Mooneys rot in jail to an indifferent California, the Scottsboro boys wait on a destiny quite outside their comprehension or control. That Miss Lonelyhearts in his great need clutches at nothing better than God is symptomatic also. As he does down in his bad luck the unsolved problems of Abandoned, Expectant and Despair must await some other deliverance.

Angel Flores: Miss Lonelyhearts in the Haunted Castle

Somebody mentioned Dostoevski and Cocteau as *Miss Lonelyhearts* progenitors. I had never seen such names coupled before. I re-read *Miss Lonelyhearts* and gradually the statement elucidated itself. In *Miss Lonelyhearts* do appear the hairshirts worn by Fyodor's heroes, and the air rings with antiChristian catapults, bloody guffaws and mystical quavers. The author of *Miss Lonely-*

"Miss Lonelyhearts in the Haunted Castle" by Angel Flores. From Contempo *3 (July 25, 1933), 1. Reprinted by permission of the author.*

hearts has not tried to conceal his admiration for the Russian master. In fact the most exciting section in his earlier work, *The Dream Life of Balso Snell,* was significantly entitled *Journal of John Raskolnikov Gilson.* Dostoevski *is* a concomitant of *Miss Lonelyhearts*—but how about Cocteau? I did not see the point clearly perhaps because Cocteau has so many sides and the side my friend had in mind was not predominantly Cocteauan. What my friend really meant was that peculiar nightmarish quality, that pervasive uncanniness which hovers over the canvasses of Giorgio de Chirico and Salvador Dalí. In literature it existed, coarsely, in the terrorists of the XVIIIth century, in the Walpole-Reeve-Rad- cliffe trio, and, more particularly, in Lewis' *The Monk.* Later it entered the chapel of the Symbolists via Poe-Coleridge, and now reigns, stylized, in surrealisme, Mystery saturates the finest works of the day. Ribemont-Dessaignes Jouhandeau, René Char, Péret, Desnos, and to a lesser degree, Drieu la Rochelle and Henri Pou- laille. And though at some distance from, say, *Confiteor*—one can sense it in such vastly different creations as *Der Steppenwolf* and *Geheimnis eines Menschen* . . .

Nathanael West's most remarkable performance has been to bring Fyodor's dark angels into the Haunted Castle. He did not recurr to the drab realism which is so responsible for the stagnation in the works of the younger American writers—a realism which gen- erally produces accurate reporting, easy-to-handle bulletins and timetables, and ALSO bad literature. Mr. West has given us an- guish and terror and fantasy (Dostoevski-Ribemont-Dessaignes?) at the very crucial moment when the current vanguard taste insists on directing literature towards the casehistory, gravymashpotato tradition.

William Carlos Williams: Sordid? Good God!

It's not only in the news section but among the feature sections also that newspapers show they have been published to conceal

Contempo *3, no. 11 (July 25, 1933): 5, 8. All Rights Reserved. Reprinted by permission of New Directions Publishing Corporation, agents for Mrs. William Carlos Williams.*

the news. West takes for his theme "The Miss Lonelyhearts of The New York *Post-Dispatch* (Are-you-in-trouble? Do-you-need-advice? Write-to-Miss-Lonelyhearts-and-she-will-help-you)." It is of course a man who runs the column.

Now this is a particularly sordid piece of business, this sort of feature, for it must be obvious that no serious advice can be given to despairing people who would patronize and even rely on such a newspaper office. The fact is that the newspaper by this means capitalizes misfortune to make sales, offering a pitiful moment's interest to the causal reader while it can do nothing but laugh at those who give it their trust.

Imagine a sensitive man running such a column, a man of imagination who realizes what he is doing and the plot is wound up. What cure? Why the only cure, so far as Nathanael West is concerned, the only truth possible is "the truth"—along with the effects of the evil upon his protagonist. A particularly interesting short novel.

And for this, because the subject matter is sometimes rather stiff, a critic (after all, one must call them something) writing in one of our daily papers has branded the book itself as "sordid." Good God.

How much longer will it take, I wonder, for America to build up a cultural ice of sufficient thickness to bear a really first rate native author? It will happen sooner or later, it must, for we already have a few excellent craftsmen. But—to paraphrase the late Bert Williams—when? Apparently we still make the old and puerile error of finding a work, because its subject matter is unsmiling, serious or if the matter smiles then naturally the book must be light. And so, taking a sordid truth of city making and carrying the facts of the case through to an engrossing climax in brilliant fashion, the book cannot be anything else but sordid also!

If this is so, why then so is *Macbeth* sordid, so *Crime and Punishment,* so nearly the whole of Greek tragedy. And so's your old man. Blah. And that's what our standard American criticism amounts to: Roxy and the statues. Thin ice. We fall through it into mud up to our knees. And there is scarcely a place we can turn to for relief.

This isn't a perfect book, few first books are. But it is excellently conceived and written and it cannot be thrust aside in such slip-shod fashion. There are many reasons why nearly everyone who would pick it up would enjoy it.

One thing which has perhaps aided in a careless dismissal of the book is West's insistence on extreme types in his narrative—really the people that newspapers do get letters from: the girl without a nose, the simpleminded child who was raped on the roof of a tenement, "Sick-of-it-all," "Broken-hearted," "Desperate," "Disillu-sioned-with-tubercular-husband." But after all the use of such extreme types is pre-eminently the business of literature or we should never have had either Romeo and Juliet, Klytemnestra or Lazarus, whose function it has been to reveal and emphasize a point under observation from a logical intelligence of the facts. Even Betty the innocent if battered girl of the story must be carried down by this dreadful logic also. The fact that she does not become hard-boiled to the end being in itself an interesting sidelight on West's objective.

The letters-to-the-papers which West uses freely and at length must be authentic. I can't believe anything else. The unsuspected world they reveal is beyond ordinary thought. They are a terrific commentary on our daily lack of depth in thought of others. Should such lives as these letters reveal never have been brought to light? Should such people, like the worst of our war wounded, best be kept in hiding?

The characters in West's book, these people whom the news-papers make a business of deceiving, are the direct incentive to his story, the seriously injured of our civic life—although the cases occur everywhere, even worse, perhaps, in the rural districts. The unbearable letters are cited and then the moral bludgeoning which they entail is rapidly sketched out before our eyes. Nothing more clearly upon the track of classical precedent.

If our thought would evade such matters West doesn't. But it is done with skill and virtuosity. It can skate. What is the figure than Dante uses in the Inferno? It is Virgil. It is poetry (that is, good writing) which permits a man, but no ordinary man, to descend to those regions for a purpose. It is the art of writing, in other words, which permits the downward motion since when writing is well made it enlivens and elevates the whole reader—without sweetening or benumbing the sense—while he plunges toward catastrophy.

I'm not dragging in Dante to say West writes poetic prose. He doesn't. But I am saying the book is written with skill, we are not wiped around by sloppy narrative. The story, dreadful as it is, is presented tolerably to us, do what we may about the things presented. It's no treatise, no cold dissection. It is the intelligence feelingly going beside us to make it possible for us at the very least to look and to understand.

> Although Mary always grunted and upset her eyes, she would not associate what she felt with the sexual act. When he forced this association, she became very angry. He had been convinced that her grunts were genuine by the change that took place in her when he kissed her heavily. Then her body gave off an odor that enriched the synthetic flower scent she used behind her ears and in the hollows of her neck. . . . He found himself in the window of a pawnshop full of fur coats, diamond rings, watches, shotguns, fishing tackle, mandolins. All these were the paraphernalia of suffering. . . . Perhaps I can make you understand. Let's start from the beginning. A man is hired to give advice to the readers of a newspaper. The job is a circulation stunt and the whole staff considers it a joke. He welcomes the job, for it might lead to a gossip column, and anyway he's tired of being a leg man. He too considers the job a joke, but after several months of it, the joke begins to escape him. He sees the majority of the letters are profoundly humble pleas for moral and spiritual advice, that they are inarticulate expressions of genuine suffering. He also discovers that the correspondents take him seriously. For the first time in his life, he is forced to examine the values by which he lives. This examination shows him that he is the victim of the joke and not its perpetrator.
>
> Then someone started a train of stories by suggesting that what they all needed was a good rape.
>
> "I knew a gal who was regular until she fell in with a group and went literary. She began writing for the little magazines about how much Beauty hurt her and dished the boy friend who set up pins in a bowling alley. The guys on the block got sore and took her into the lots one night. About eight of them. They ganged her proper."

Take it or leave it. It's impossible to quote effectively for anything but a minor purpose but that's approximately what the prose is like. It's plain American. What I should like to show is that West has a fine feeling for language. And this is the point I shall stop on. Anyone using American must have taste in order to be able to select from among the teeming vulgarisms of our speech the personal and telling vocabulary which he needs to put over his effects. West possesses this taste.

Chronology of Important Dates

	Nathanael West	The Age
1903	(October) West born, New York City.	"George Orwell" born; Ford Motor Company founded.
1910		James G. Frazer, *Totemism and Exogamy;* Edwin Arlington Robinson, *The Town Down the River.*
1913		Sigmund Freud, *Totem and Taboo;* Wolfgang Köhler, *Gestalt Theory.*
1915		Edgar Lee Masters, *Spoon River Anthology.*
1917		T. S. Eliot, *Prufrock and Other Observations.*
1921		Eliot, *The Waste Land.*
1922	(Autumn) Enters and leaves Tufts University, enrolls at Brown University.	James Joyce, *Ulysses.*
1924	(June) Graduates from Brown.	Ernest Hemingway, *In Our Time;* André Breton's Surrealist manifesto in Paris
1924–1925	In Paris.	
1925		William Carlos Williams, *In the American Grain;* John Dos Passos, *Manhattan transfer;* F. Scott Fitzgerald, *The Great Gatsby;* e. e. cummings, *XLI Poems*

1926		Hemingway, *The Sun Also Rises;* R. H. Tawney, *Religion and the Rise of Capitalism;* Chiang Kai-shek fighting in Chinese Civil War; Rudolph Valentino dies
1927	Working at Sutton and Kenmore Hotels, New York City. Meets James T. Farrell, William Carlos Williams, and other literary figures.	Lindbergh flies Atlantic; Sacco-Vanzetti case.
1928		Williams, *A Voyage to Pagany;* Ezra Pound, *Cantos* 17–27.
1929		Wall Street crash; Hemingway, *A Farewell to Arms;* Thomas Wolfe, *Look Homeward, Angel.*
1930		Hart Crane, *The Bridge;* José Ortega y Gasset, *The Revolt of the Masses;* Freud, *Civilization and its Discontents;* massive unemployment.
1931	*The Dream Life of Balso Snell.*	Eugene O'Neill, *Mourning Becomes Electra;* William Faulkner, *Sanctuary.*
1932	Edits *Contact* with Williams; meets Josephine Herbst.	Faulkner, *Light in August;* Erskine Caldwell, *Tobacco Road.*
1933	Publishes *Miss Lonelyhearts;* living on farm in Erwinna, Pennsylvania, near Josephine Herbst and husband.	Franklin D. Roosevelt inaugurated; Adolf Hitler Chancellor in Germany; Pound, *A Draft of XXX Cantos;* end of Prohibition; Archibald MacLeish, *Frescoes for Mr. Rockefeller's City.*

1934	(June *A Cool Million*.	Henry Miller, *Tropic of Cancer;* André Breton, *What is Surrealism?* Lewis Mumford, *Technics and Civilization*.
1935	Arrested in picket line in New York City; development of leftist political views; in summer, working as writer at Republic Studios, signs American Writers Congress manifesto.	Manifesto of American Writers Congress; Pound, *Make it New;* John Steinbeck, *Tortilla Flat;* Soviet purge trials; Wagner Act signed; building of Boulder Dam.
1936		Army mutinies in Spain, Civil War begins; Italy conquers Ethiopia; Dos Passos, *The Big Money;* Faulkner, *Absalom, Absalom!*
1938	Collaborates on two unsuccessful plays.	*Anschluss;* Cummings, *Collected Poems;* Jean-Paul Sartre, *Nausée;* Orson Welles' radio play of invasion from Mars creates panic in United States; Williams, *Collected Poems*.
1939	*The Day of the Locust*	World War II begins; Yeats, Freud die; Steinbeck, *The Grapes of Wrath*.
1940	(April) Married to Eileen McKenney. (December) West and his wife die in an auto accident.	F. Scott Fitzgerald dies; Hemingway, *For Whom the Bell Tolls;* Eliot, "East Coker"; Richard Wright, *Native Son;* Trotsky murdered.

Notes on the Editor and Contributors

THOMAS H. JACKSON, the editor of this collection, is Associate Professor of English at Bryn Mawr College. He has written a study of the early poetry of Ezra Pound and is currently working on a book on early twentieth-century poetry.

ROBERT ANDREACH teaches English at Harpur College in New York. He has written on Henry James and on Eugene O'Neill, and published *Studies in Structure* in 1964.

ARTHUR M. COHEN's careers have comprised both writing and publishing. His books include *Martin Buber, Religion and Contemporary Society,* and *The Myth of the Judeo-Christian Tradition;* he was the founder of the Noonday Press, and is president of Meridian Books.

ROBERT I. EDENBAUM is associate Professor of English at Temple University. He has published on John Hawkes, Dashiell Hammett—and Delacroix.

ANGEL FLORES, a contemporary of West's, is an energetic and prolific translator, editor, and critic of many foreign literatures. He has translated German, French, Spanish, and Italian poetry, and has done critical works on Kafka and Lope de Vega.

JOSEPHINE HERBST, who died in 1969, had a long career in American letters and was in touch with many of the most active and creative American writers of our time. The author of several novels, she also wrote a book on John Bartram and the early American naturalists, *New Green World,* in 1954. Her work was always marked by great warmth and generosity of spirit.

STANLEY EDGAR HYMAN, who taught for many years at Bennington College, was the author of some seven books and editor of more. Perhaps his best-known books continue to be *The Armed Vision,* a survey of modern criticism, and its companion anthology, *The Critical Performance.*

JAMES F. LIGHT is Bernhard Professor and Chairman of the Department of English at the University of Bridgeport. In addition to *Nathanael West: An Interpretative Study,* he has written on John William De Forest and co-edited a book called *The Modern Age;* he has published articles on Hemingway, Fitzgerald, and De Forest.

RANDALL REID, a Californian and a Stanford Ph.D., has taught at San Diego State College and Deep Springs College, and now teaches English and humanities at the University of Chicago.

EDMOND L. VOLPE has just retired as chairman of the English department at New York's City College. A specialist on Henry James and modern American literature, he wrote *Reader's Guide to Faulkner* in 1964 and co-edited *Ten Modern Short Novels.*

WILLIAM CARLOS WILLIAMS was among the major American poets of this century. Deeply committed to the life and practice of American literary culture, he needs no introduction here.

Selected Bibliography

Comerchero, Victor, *Nathanael West, The Ironic Prophet* (Syracuse: Syracuse University Press, 1964), Chap. 5. A thorough discussion of the ironic in *Miss Lonelyhearts;* heavily weighted toward Freudian psychology and mythology.

Lorch, Thomas M., "West's *Miss Lonelyhearts:* Skepticism Mitigated?" *Renascence* 18 (Winter, 1966), 99–109. Discusses the influence of Starbuck and William James on the religious theme in *Miss Lonelyhearts.* Lorch sees West's hero as tapping the "vital reality and force" of religious mysticism: ". . . West suggests that religion may be a positive source of insight and creativity as well as a destructive illusion."

Martin, Jay, *Nathanael West, The Art of His Life* (New York: Farrar Straus & Giroux, Inc., 1970). A more recent and compendious biography than Light's, but neither quite replaces the other.

Podhoretz, Norman, "A Particular Kind of Joking," *New Yorker* 33 (May 18, 1957), 156–65. A review of *The Complete Works of Nathanael West* (New York: Farrar, Straus, and Cudahy, 1957); an interesting and useful attempt to furnish an overall rationale for West's work, this review sees West as a writer of "high comedy" and draws attention to the apolitical negativism of his writing.

Ratner, Marc L., " 'Anywhere Out of this World': Baudelaire and Nathanael West," *American Literature* 31 (January, 1960), 456–63. Ties the "central experience" of *Miss Lonelyhearts* to Baudelaire's prose-poem "N'importe Où Hors du Monde." Sees Miss Lonelyhearts as more successful with his inner life than the text would seem to warrant, but an interesting essay.

Reid, Randall, *The Fiction of Nathanael West* (Chicago and London: The University of Chicago Press, 1967). Easily the best critical study of West's work extant; a highly suggestive, if overdrawn, study of the intellectual and literary backgrounds of West's work, and a sound critical reading of the entire *oeuvre*.

Ross, Alan, "Novelist–Philosophers: XIV—The Dead Center: An Introduction to Nathanael West," *Horizon* 18 (October, 1948), 248–96. Reprinted in *The Complete Works of Nathanael West*. A useful, though necessarily general, survey of the broader issues in West's novels.

Schwartz, Edward Greenfield, "The Novels of Nathanael West," *Accent* 17 (Autumn, 1957), 251–62. Another review of *The Complete Works;* like Ross's and Podhoretz's, necessarily general, but a useful tracing of themes and preoccupations throughout West's career, pointing out his limitations as well as his virtues.

Tibbetts, A. M., "The Strange Half-World of Nathanael West," *Prairie Schooner* 34 (Spring, 1960), 8–12. A not altogether successful discussion of some of West's weaknesses; despite its pedestrian style and thought, however, this article raises issues whose confrontation is useful to the reader of West's books.

TWENTIETH CENTURY
INTERPRETATIONS

MAYNARD MACK, *Series Editor*
Yale University

NOW AVAILABLE
Collections of Critical Essays
ON

(continued on next page)

(*continued from previous page*)

TWENTIETH CENTURY VIEWS

American Authors